PARSON'S SAMPLER

PARSON'S SAMPLER

Patterns whereby Words
Become the Language of Power

JAMES W. KENNEDY

THE PILGRIM PRESS

BOSTON

PRINTED IN THE UNITED STATES OF AMERICA

TO MY FATHER

Whose patient, understanding love
allowed God's way with a son

A MORE EFFECTIVE MINISTRY

CHRISTIAN EVANGELISM is the permanent occupation of the Church. Today, as in apostolic times, the word spoken in season and out of season is the means whereby the Church grows and expands in membership; but the peculiar feature of our times is the wide variety of different ways in which that word, spoken both in season and out of season, now finds expression. The great opportunity for preaching the Christian message which existed in the first century is now matched by an equal variety of possible methods. The Christian preacher of today has not only his pulpit as a place where he can preach a sermon or two each week. He also has a dozen other channels through which he can send his message. In the first place, there is the radio. In addition to the congregation before him in the parish church, his sermon may be broadcast to many listeners outside. More than that, he may preach once a week or even daily on a " church of the air " program. Add to this all manner of public occasions in the life of the community — in the public schools, at luncheons and dinners of various organizations, clubs, and societies (not all of them with a primarily religious purpose). There is also the church school and various organizations in the parish, where plays, pageants, and other dramatic performances are produced from time to time. Then there is the Children's Church or the Junior Church, where the clergyman has a wonderful opportunity to preach the Christian message to receptive minds and sow the seed of Christian faith. Finally, add to all this the range of opportunity which lies open before the clergyman who knows how to write, who can produce essays, poems, literary or historical articles — not to overlook the vast and growing field of fiction. In brief, if a clergyman sets out to take advantage of all his opportunities, he will need most of twenty-four hours a day!

And it is a twenty-four-hour-a-day job, being a minister; for the evangelistic side of his ministry is balanced by the pastoral, educational, and liturgical. The old-fashioned, dignified peace and quiet of the Victorian manse or rectory no longer exists. If a parson is any good at all, he is probably on his job every minute of every day. Like a good doctor, he has more " calls " than he can take care of — both calls to be made on the sick and the needy, and also calls that come by telephone.

It is difficult to describe the various techniques of evangelism which are available to the clergy of the present day. Better than any description is an actual demonstration. Since most of us " learn by doing," it is a wise plan for the young clergyman to serve as curate or assistant minister in a parish headed by such a man as the author of this book. Mr. Kennedy makes effective use, not only of his pulpit in Christ Church, Lexington, Kentucky, but of a dozen other media for preaching the Christian gospel. Next to studying with him at first hand, the reading of this book will enable the reader to recognize — and apply to his own situation — something of the range and variety of available media for present-day evangelism. The material presented in the following pages is not meant to be " lifted," or even " adapted " and used elsewhere. Canned sermons are like canned fruit, never as good as the ripe fruit fresh from the orchard. What Mr. Kennedy has presented is a series of samples of what can be done, illustrations of various methods of doing it, and suggestions that may strike fire in other men's minds. There is nothing presumptuous about this any more than there is in a surgeon lecturing to his fellows in a clinic, or an artist explaining to other members of his craft how he goes about his work. Nor is there anything peculiarly

denominational about this book. The author is an Episcopalian, but his book is for all the churches. I am confident
that ministers in many different places, in many different
kinds of places, and with many different traditions and
outlooks, will find stimulus and suggestion in this interesting
collection.

FREDERICK C. GRANT

Union Theological Seminary
New York, N. Y.

FOREWORD

Write thee all the words that I
have spoken unto thee in a book.
JEREMIAH 30:2

PARSON'S SAMPLER is an attempt to lead clergymen beyond the place where words are words to the point where they become the language of power. It is the desire of the author that the materials included in this book may furnish inspiration for the creation of each clergyman's own pattern for making Christ and his way known. No clergyman can rest until his teaching and preaching, his speaking and writing, fill the day's life with new revelations of his way.

So this book is a kind of clerical sampler, an attempt to point out some of the ways for exercising a more varied and vital ministry of words. The book is an array of special methods that may come to the help of the clergyman in meeting the endless needs of all types of men. The illustrations are the effort of an average journeyman parson to show to others, whose needs and talents are probably in the same range, methods he has found effective.

Dr. George A. Buttrick once said to a group of clergymen, "The two most powerful forces on earth are the written word and the spoken word. Therefore if you have talent for writing acceptably for publication use it; and if you have the voice and the interest for the very special and unlimited channel of radio, use it to the utmost." These words are as I remember them, and they have inspired me ever since to work hard at developing whatever gifts God has given me for the spread of his kingdom.

Psychologists now know from recent studies made of college students that they learn only about one-tenth of what they are capable of learning. I believe the same figures would apply to the clergy: we are only about one-tenth as effective as we could be.

Most of us deal in sermonic fashion with everything we write or say. The deliberate aim of this book is to open up many non-sermonic ways of writing and speaking which carry the good news in different ways to different groups of people at possible points of contact often ignored. We have set up an ideal, to be sure, but when we dream about it and work, work, work to reach it, the dream may emerge as realized fact. We strive so that we may not forever " heap up empty phrases." (Matthew 6:7) If we read and think awhile upon the words, and pray for new strength and vision, we may discover wider fields for our talents.

JAMES W. KENNEDY

ACKNOWLEDGMENTS

THE AUTHOR wishes to acknowledge his indebtedness to a host of unknown writers and publishers for inspiration and ideas which have been of inestimable help through the years. Several of the items brought together in this book were first published in the following periodicals: The Churchman, The Southern Churchman, The Church Review, The Texas Churchman, Religion in Life, The Pastor, The Presbyterian of the South. Other parts of the book were broadcast by the author in various radio programs, including Mutual's Radio Chapel, The Episcopal Hour, Haven, and "Parson Jim."

The Cloister Press graciously extended permission to reprint "Hey Buddy." And we appreciate the courtesy of Thomas Nelson and Sons for permission to use quotations from the Revised Standard Version of the New Testament.

The author also wishes to express special gratitude to Richard A. Newhouse for suggestions concerning revision of the manuscript; to Mrs. Keith Koenig for assistance in preparation of the manuscript; and to Frances, his wife, without whose objective and devoted guidance much of what appears in the book might never have been written.

J. W. K.

CONTENTS

CHAPTER I

THE MAN AND HIS SERMON

They shall speak with new tongues.

MARK 16:17

THE WRITING of sermons is quite a familiar process to all of us. Every clergyman is in the midst of sermon preparation from the moment he learns the magic of text, introduction, points one, two and three, and conclusion in his homiletics course. Practically all of us try to squeeze ourselves at first into someone else's special pattern, which does not fit us. My professor at the seminary was a great preacher, but all he tried to teach us was how *he* did it — the way he gathered and filed material, put it together and delivered it (complete with gestures) to his large congregation. It was a great moment of relief, revelation, and release when I discovered that I did not have to try to become another George Craig Stewart, which of course was impossible anyhow. From that moment of realization, I began to strive to become freely and completely the individual God created, developing whatever preaching potential I had, and recognizing certain limitations which were also mine.

This subject has been covered many times by abler minds. All I want to do is to put before you a few samples of sermons which have been preached and in part have found lodgment in the hearts of some of those who heard.

Let us read together a few sermons of a general nature first, looking, not for the flaws which will most surely be found, but for new ideas, different angles of treatment, any useful hints for enriching or improving one's own sermon technique.

Christian Worship — An Adventure

The whole question of worship is one which should be at the center of our thoughts more frequently. So let us delve into the subject with the hope that a new and true concept of worship may result.

Here are some of the things that have come to us about Christian worship, which is, in its purity, a thrilling adventure. The ready-made text is in Matthew 15:8-9 from *An American Translation* [1]: "This people honor me with their lips, yet their hearts are far away from me . . . (therefore) their worship of me is all in vain." Does this not explain why so many people leave God's house every Sunday exactly as they came: with their same old worries, fears, pettinesses, irritations, burdens, grudges, ill-will, soured dispositions, unloving natures? God knows why they keep on coming! Perhaps it is something more than habit; perhaps it is because of some unknown yearning or unsatisfied desire. But their worship is sterile and vain. We know this because nothing happens. In fact, they do not worship at all, or the aforementioned fears and sins could not remain.

Matthew gets this text passage from the prophet Isaiah (29:13). Now Isaiah knew how to worship. He recorded one of his tremendous experiences of worship in God's house, and we may summarize his words thus: "I saw the Lord . . . I heard his voice . . . He sent me forth." That is the sum and substance of real worship. So there is need for us to reconsider the meaning of worship from time to time lest its pristine power be lost to us. Since worship is at the heart of all the life and witness of the church, it must be related specifically to the life and needs of men.

[1] From *The Bible, An American Translation*, by Smith and Goodspeed. Used by permission of the University of Chicago Press.

No one who speaks on worship can afford to ignore Evelyn Underhill's masterly contribution to the subject. She says, " in its deepest sense, it is the response of man to the Eternal." [1] *Response* is the important word here. It means the act of responding in answer to a stimulus. We can respond to something only when we have been stimulated by it in some way. The place where we worship is not particularly important, just so long as something happens, because " no matter where man worships he comes there to procure the love of God " for use in the world of men. How important it is to stir up our minds and wills occasionally in order to examine the essential meaning of worship for us! We must align our thoughts about the matter and realize that real worship consists only in the humble beginnings of man's response to the attraction of God — the birth of faith, hope, and love, and all each one implies.

Since worship means the priority of God in all things, then Christian worship must consist of a twofold movement — upward to God and downward into human activity. Worship impels us again and again into the world, full of the inspired power to live a life which is closer to God. It hardens the will to live righteously into an action pattern; to do, to be, for Christ's sake; and the whole man is involved. Not lips alone but hearts as well.

Worship, then, is the conscious recognition of God as the beginning and end of life. We should be reminded of this every time we see the symbols Alpha and Omega — the symbol of God as the beginning and the ending of all things. If this be true is not the criterion for any service of worship: " Does it help to bring God near? " If it does not, it is not sufficient stimulus to gain man's response, and no action will

[1] From *Worship*, by Evelyn Underhill. Harper & Brothers, publishers. Used by permission.

ensue. But beware of the ever-present temptation to blame the service or the sermon for the lack of response. When we are ready for God to enter our hearts and minds and speak to us, he always manages to ignite a spark from some thought or feeling.

By now there should be no doubt in anyone's mind about the meaning of worship, but what of the implications? At the outset, we declared that Christian worship is an adventure. By this we mean that in its literal sense of appearing worthily in God's presence, it is an adventure in its literal sense of that which happens. Look, then, at what worship meant to Jesus, in order to get at its root meaning. Jesus worshiped in synagogue and Temple. In the latter there were wonderfully beautiful and impressive services, with rich pageantry and colorful processions and ritual. But Jesus found that the services had lost some of the primitive reality of contact with God which the psalmists had sung into his heart. The services were thrilling, yes, but God was completely hidden by the observance of laws and the making of sacrifices, and by the infrequent attendance upon the great Temple services — for most of the people it was once a year, at the time of the Feast of the Passover. The letter of worship was there, every dotted i and crossed t of it. But the spirit was largely missing and therefore so was the response. The Father's house was no longer the same house of prayer in which Isaiah had worshiped. No longer was his experience relived: " I saw the Lord . . . I heard his voice . . . He sent me forth."

So far as the reality of God was concerned, Temple worship was thoroughly decadent in the time of Christ. He worshiped in both the Temple and the synagogues, but he tried to give new content and meaning to the letter of the law. He wanted it to be fulfilled and not to stagnate for lack of forward and upward movement. He gave God to those who really wanted him and opened the long-closed avenue leading back to the great worship experiences of Isaiah, Jeremiah, and some of the psalmists, and leading forward to even greater moments of response and dedication.

Worship became for Jesus and the apostles something very real and intimate and wonderful. God was in their midst, and look what their worship prompted them to do! To go forth, ever farther from the center, declaring the good news, doing good works, never ceasing to serve man through the empowering impulse of worship. This was for them a stirring adventure. It was dangerous. It was rewarding. Something was always happening through it. This fellowship set the pattern for worship in the early church, which was the simple and yet complete response through the " breaking of bread " and " spiritual exercises." They came together to pray and remember and to give thanks with "psalms, hymns and sacred songs." They did not bother much about the form. They were concerned mainly with the two elements that always seemed to be present — joy and reality. God was real and in the midst of them because Christ was central and in the midst of them. They knew he would always be present in some way. Therefore they approached their fellowship services together with great and joyful expectations. Their worship must have meant something tremendous, for they risked death and imprisonment to come together. Because Christ was living and central and real, through him God was living and central and real. Too often our liturgies have imprisoned him. The cross was and is central to Christian worship. It is the symbol of release through self-offering. It was and is Jesus' complete response to God. We keep it central in order to make prompt our response to God's kind of love, which gave all, that we might see the way to a free and abundant life. It will so prompt us when we give ourselves up to it; that is, when we allow God's spirit to infuse us and motivate us. Then we too will report of our worship: " I saw the Lord . . . I heard his voice . . . He sent me forth."

Paul's admonition to the Athenians concerning their ignorant worship of an unknown God is strangely apt sometimes in describing our worship. God is largely unknown to some of us, or so we must assume, for there seems to be no response to him. No wonder people are not won over to church attendance when we who worship so often do not always show the far-reaching results of our worshiping. Perhaps they too read the inscription indicative of our worship — " To an unknown God." Paul might admonish any group of worshipers today and say: " Wanton creatures," you have denied God's existence because your response is not worthy . . . indeed, it is nil. We must never forget the centrality of the response, that which we allow to happen to us in God's presence. And it is always a person's response to God which strengthens, renews, and enlightens us. If we respond to the thousand and one little things that we sometimes allow to disturb and annoy us, we will find that both reality and joy have been driven out. Life actually becomes different as we truly worship, for worship is the sure cure for our petty bickerings and concerns over this, that, and the other thing. It should drive all else but God from our hearts and minds. How can we remain the same little selves, following our worship, as we were before our worship, if we really worship in the true sense of that tremendous word? If we come seeking to procure the love of God for living more completely his plan for us, we will get it, and the petty concerns of our smaller selves will fall into their own insignificant places and be swallowed up or forgotten.

We could define worship again and again and quote the

experiences and beliefs of great persons concerning it, but we can never know the meaning of it until this question is answered: What does worship mean to you and to me? Does it cause anything to happen? Is it a joyful adventure? Can anyone tell by the way we look and act that we have worshiped? Are we inspired and equipped to go forth and serve Him, regardless of consequences?

The conclusion of every service of worship should witness a love feast of righted wrongs and restored relationships; of family and community changes. One should leave cleansed, strengthened, renewed, whole every whit. The congregation should be eagerly comparing notes on the discoveries made in God's presence and the impulse to live them out. God does not want lip service but closeness of heart and mind. God wants a response. God wants us to do something for him . . . "ceaseless self-offering to the increase of the glory of God." When this happens in a church, the world will beat a path to its doors and the God of Jesus Christ will be brought near, and man will desire nothing more than to live out life in his service, which is the only perfect freedom. The church will then make its power felt in the life of men, and stand strong for every truth of God, and track injustice to its lair.

Christian worship can indeed be an adventure; because it is the reaching up after enough of God's Spirit to make life work according to his plan, using it for hastening our growth toward oneness with Christ's victorious life.

Each time we come to any moment of worship, be it daily alone or on Sundays in God's house, the joy and reality, the definite pattern of response experienced by Isaiah should be ours. " I saw the Lord," I was conscious of his presence, I knew he was near. " I heard his voice," I was aware of an inner stirring. " He sent me forth," to live at my highest level of response to the eternal verity of love.

As we worship — respond to God — things will happen,
life will move, and noble souls will walk the earth, in tune
with his spirit, at work for his kingdom.

Collision: A Law of God

A brief introductory lesson and text from Paul's letter
to the Philippians:

"Whatever happens, show yourselves citizens worthy of
the good news of the Christ, so that whether I come and see
you or am kept away and only hear news of you, I may
know that you are standing firm with one spirit, one purpose, fighting side by side for faith in the good news. Never
for a moment falter before your opponents, for your fear-
lessness will be a sure sign for them of their coming destruction, but to you it will be an omen from God himself
of your deliverance. For you have been granted the privilege not only of trusting in Christ but of suffering for him.
Take your part in the same struggle that you have seen me
engage in and that you hear I am still keeping up." (Philippians 1:27-30)[1]

The sermon subject today is Collision: a law of God, a
philosophy of crisis. What do we mean by "collision, a law
of God"? Just this, that when two or more things or
principles come together, that is, collide or encounter one
another, one, the weaker, must always succumb to the other,
the stronger. We might add that when collision occurs
between two equal forces, nothing happens except an im-
passe. What do we mean by saying that "collision is a
philosophy of crisis"? Simply this: that collision, which
means to come up strongly against, is a method of dealing

---

[1] From *The Bible, An American Translation,* by Smith and Goodspeed.
Used by permission of the University of Chicago Press.

with crisis; it is the method that Christ used; it is the method that we can use.

It always seemed to me a little out of place to see advertisements some years ago in magazines showing football helmets and mattresses on the ends of boxcars, which were supposed to absorb the jolt when the cars knocked against other boxcars. Needless to say, these advertisements were not illustrative of the Christian religion. Collision is a law of God and there are no easy cushions to take all of the jolt away.

Collision is a daily demand on all Christians. Desire is always colliding with love. Selfishness is always colliding with sacrifice. The present or the past is always colliding with the future. And one of these must prevail, if there is to be continued movement. If they are of equal strength, nothing happens and we stop. We are not interested in anything beyond the spiritual collisions or conflicts which develop when such opposites as have been mentioned are on the same track and therefore will inevitably collide.

But *first* we might consider some avoidance of collisions, or softening of collisions, and what results.

We know now, since they have been published, that the facts in the existing situation before Pearl Harbor and the fall of Singapore were not " collided with." In the report we find all sorts of things but the facing of issues squarely — the admission that the truth was thus and so. There was apparently no attempt and no inclination to meet truth head on, and the results were a tragic debacle. Then there is the unforgettable Scarlett O'Hara, who always used the technique of putting off the collision until tomorrow, because the collision seemed very easy to meet tomorrow — that is, from today's vantage point. We always think how brave we'll be tomorrow. And there was Nicodemus, who refused to collide with the opinion of his day and sought Jesus by night. Those who would compromise or procrastinate keep on the side which demands no collision, because it seems the easiest thing to do at the moment.

Stone walls are hard, and few there are of us who are willing to hit them head on, and so we go along the side and try to find a space where the wall is broken down. We know that truth and reality hurt and we do not want to come up against them. That is why men evade issues of importance until they are cornered and have to face them, and then they awkwardly and weakly make a stand with too little — often too late.

Men avoid head-on encounter because it hurts, and their excuse is that this pain is unnecessary, that it saps too much of their strength, and that if they conserve their strength they will be able to make a better stand later on. That may be good strategically in battle sometimes but never in battles of the spirit. It is strange how the history of much of man-kind has been the history of following the path of least resistance. We find it difficult, after sensing what others are thinking and what they will think of us if we go against their fixed opinions, to do anything more than conform. This means we are guided by them and not by what is right. Yes, there are too few bold stands because of fear of criti-cism or isolation from a group.

You remember those Christians in the early days who did not obey the injunction of Paul to the Philippians; they burned incense to the emperor; they couldn't come head on; they did not believe strongly enough.

So there are many examples of ways in which we avoid collision. But there are also innumerable examples in which we come up against something and collide with it squarely; and the results from these collisions are very illuminating and startling.

You remember the incident when Peter and John were

hauled up before the magistrate who said, " You can't preach about this man, you can't talk about him — he is dangerous," and how they laughed at the magistrate then and said, " We cannot obey you — we have to obey God, and if it means coming up against hard things, well, that is unfortunate but there is nothing we can do about it — we must obey God rather than man." And there was young Stephen, who knew he was going to get his head bashed in — who knew he was going to be killed for what he said; and yet, he had to say it; it was the truth and so he spoke it, and he was unflinching before that which came. Then take Jeremiah — you remember the terrible struggle he had between what he desired to do or not to do and his sense of duty. God finally convinced him that he had a mission to perform, and so he went against every feeling that he had. He wanted to get out of it, but he did not; he came up against it because he knew that was what he should do.

In an issue of *Time* during the Second World War there was the story of some of the great and noble clergy of Norway coming head on with the Nazis because of what they believed, and their bishop and many others going to prison because of it. Yet, during their imprisonment and later after the war, their influence was much greater than ever before. They went to prison — and some to death — but they were free and are free. It is still possible that these men will dominate the world to come in that part of the earth. All of these were men of God, men like Isaiah and Jeremiah and Amos and all the rest — men who collided, who came head on, with all the social and personal and national standards or issues which were contrary to the commands and laws of God, men who made no compromise with evil.

Jesus himself was always having to come up against the customs or the laws or the traditions of his times, and over and over again he had to collide head on with them. That is why the Pharisees sought to kill him; that is why he lost his life. His law was of God. This was first. All were rebels then who collided with tradition, man-made laws, authorities other than God. They bore personal witness to the law of collision. They proved what happens when a live soul collides with a dead soul: that life is changed, is given point and purpose, is knocked out of a negative do-nothing state, is made creative and begins to grow. Our problems and issues today must be met even if we have to collide head on with them in a clear-cut witnessing to our belief in the truth — and there can only be one truth — the way of God for us.

So there are those of us who collide and those of us who evade collision, and the question is, how are we to follow those who are the colliders and to avoid those who are the dodgers?

Certain of our hymns inspire us in this matter. Take, for example, that magnificent hymn, " Once to every man and nation comes the moment to decide," and another hymn, " He who would valiant be 'gainst all disaster, let him in constancy follow the Master"; both are illustrative of hymns that show us how men empowered with Christ's spirit cannot dodge issues, if those issues are contrary to what they believe is right and true.

All children love to read stories about dragons, but the stories must have knights in shining armor who go out and kill the dragons. Children always root for the knight because they know the dragon will have a vulnerable spot, and that when the knight goes out and meets the beast, the dragon will always be vanquished. Well, isn't it true that no terror — represented by the dragon — is vanquished until it comes head on with a truth or a faith that is willing to tackle it — that is, the knight?

Or take the story of David and Goliath. This story

thrilled me so much that I used to practice with a slingshot by the hour. I too wanted to kill giants with little smooth stones and a nice slingshot. David was a wonderful chap and I never tired of listening over and over again to his killing of Goliath. But we have never yet known a Goliath to be killed until someone took the weapons at hand and went out to encounter him.

You remember the Lord's Prayer, where it says, " Lead us not into temptation, but deliver us from evil " ? This means that we will never be led into temptation, if we confront temptation and meet it on its own ground, with the power of Christ behind us. And he will always deliver us from evil, if we will depend upon him. Evil can have dominion over us and win us away from his way, only if we try to compromise with it. No, we must meet and vanquish it, even as the dragon or Goliath. Give no ground to evil — meet it head on — and don't put off meeting it head on; meet it *now!* For the Christian there can be no procrastination, there can be no compromise. There can be no easing around the obstacles that confront us, there can be no *slipping* into a way that is better.

Take, for a specific example, the problem of holding a Christian to the highest demands of Christ in business or industry. Failure here brings loss of power. What example has the Church offered to labor in the areas of working hours, rate of pay, sick benefits, and retirement? When right meets wrong, and we are sure of the right, we must *choose* the right. When spiritual collisions occur — that is, when two contrary principles collide — something drastic is bound to happen. When good and evil collide, one must give way or be destroyed, and the one which gives way depends upon us. Our only command: If God wants this according to what we know of his laws and plans, we must do it — without any ifs, or buts, maybe's, or halfway measures.

But when good and evil are evenly matched, how then do we gain the balance of power? The answer is simple enough, isn't it? We call upon strength from God and cease depending upon our own sword — to wrestle with evil like Job or Jacob — to use the courage God has given us and the persistence God has given us to win out.

It is true there are no cushions in life, except the cushions like the ones we have in our spinal column where there are little pads in between the bones that take up some of the jar. There are also spiritual cushions in like measure. That is why men like Paul, Amos, Hosea, Jeremiah, Christ, and others, seem not to feel the terrible blows; they seem to be happy; they seem to have resilience to their souls; and they have. It is because they possess in great measure God's love, and God's freedom, and God's forgetfulness of self.

Paul's words will furnish us with a challenge. I remind you of them and their possible application in order to cheer you, because with Paul *The Way* is always against " ways " and is always victorious over them. With Paul, God's laws are always waging war with man's laws, and winning out over them when they are in contradiction; and so perhaps we need to remember that Paul said: " Take your part in the same struggle that you have seen me engaged in, and that you may hear that I am still keeping up."

Therefore, do what Paul enjoined . . . If this law be Christ's way, it is God's law and way for me, and I will stand for it and follow it, come what may. Strong collision of good against evil results in vanquished evil and victorious good; therefore, let us remember that collision is a law of God, a philosophy of crisis for us today.

Thumbtacking Souls

" The Pin-Down " is the subject. Or we could describe it appropriately in these words, " Thumbtacking Souls."

The text is from 1 Peter 1:15: "You must be holy too in *all* your conduct;" "brace up your minds" to get that holiness (vs. 13).[1]

Have you ever thumbtacked a soul? Has your soul ever been thumbtacked or pinned down? In other words, have you ever been present when a soul (perhaps your own) was in a corner with no way to turn, except around, and must turn around if it would escape? We shall try to give a demonstration of pinning down, thumbtacking, cornering souls for everyone to see.

During my brief stay of two years in a well-known school of engineering, I made straight A+ in only one subject — mechanical drawing. I loved it and so did well with it. The success of a plate depended entirely upon how securely it was thumbtacked to the board. I do not mean this literally, of course, but all the skill in the world would have been wasted if the paper had slipped while a line was inked, or a 60-degree angle had slid arc-wise under the movement of a hard-pointed pencil to 45 degrees. Without the thumbtacks, no accuracy would have been possible, even with super instruments and good intelligence. There was no escape for the paper from the job to be done, so long as the thumb-tacks held.

In similar fashion we must pin down souls in order to get at the roots of their trouble and to draw up a plan for their redemption from aimlessness and failure.

Our method is dialogue, a fictitious conversation, but based entirely upon a true situation. The conversation begins between Soul and Thumbtack:

Thumbtack: What do you mean by the Christian religion?

Soul: Why, the religion of Christ, of course.

[1] From *The Bible, A New Translation*, by James Moffatt. Used by permission of Harper & Brothers.

Thumbtack: What denomination do you belong to?

Soul: I am an Episcopalian. (This was spoken rather proudly, implying a certain degree of thankfulness he was not something else.)

Thumbtack: Is this church the true representative of the Christian religion?

Soul: Certainly — I believe that is what we believe.

Thumbtack: Then what about the other denominations; are they not classified under the Christian religion also?

Soul: Well, perhaps. I'm sure there are some good people in them.

Thumbtack: Be more specific. Just what is the Christian religion, according to your belief as an Episcopalian?

Soul: Oh, belief in God the Father, God the Son, and God the Holy Ghost. Oh, yes, and in two major sacraments, holy communion and baptism. And I believe that is about all — oh, no, there is another thing we believe in — the Christian year.

Thumbtack: But what of Christ and his belief; what is it, according to your knowledge as an Episcopalian?

Soul: That is easy. (This time with animation and assurance.) We find it all summarized in the Lord's Prayer, the creed, and the Ten Commandments. I seem to remember something about the Sermon on the Mount too, and the Summary of the Law.

Thumbtack: Can you repeat and explain all of these?

Soul: Quite. I memorized them when I was a child. (Soul immediately rattles off the Lord's Prayer, the creed, and the Ten Commandments, and gets out the substance of the Summary of the Law, but hasn't the faintest idea of the Sermon on the Mount, where it is found, or what it contains.)

Thumbtack: If this last is the essence of Jesus' ethical teachings and, as you said in the beginning, the Christian religion is what Christ believes, how can you be a real

Christian until you have mastered what he taught in such sections of God's word as Matthew 5, 6 and 7 — the Sermon on the Mount?

Soul: But it is so long and there are so many different thoughts in it I have never found time enough to learn it.

Thumbtack (getting very intimate, almost rude): Are you then a Christian?

Soul (a bit indignantly): Most certainly.

Thumbtack: Give in a short summary sentence what it means to be a Christian.

Soul (on the instant): Follow Christ.

Thumbtack: Follow him where?

Soul: Wherever he goes, of course.

Thumbtack: How do you know where he goes and how can you be sure you are following him?

Soul: Wait a minute. This is getting too complicated. I don't have to answer these questions.

Thumbtack: No, but if you are a real Christian, you *can* answer them and will be eager to tell all you have discovered in the way of answers to them. I am not yet convinced you are a Christian. If you stop now, I'll know you are not one.

Soul (reluctantly and uneasily): Very well, then, proceed. But I can't be expected to know everything.

Thumbtack: Specifically, then, what do you know about Jesus and what has this knowledge done to you? (Thumbtack keeps insisting on details, experience, truth, real personal belief, and pins down Soul to the meaning of prayer, sin, suffering, repentance, forgiveness, God's will, worship, discipline, fellowship, the cross, self, and a host of intimate personal situations Soul has never dreamed were part of his vow as a follower of Christ.)

At long last, a thoroughly humbled Soul was pinned down to the point of discovery and admission and knelt with Thumbtack and prayed this prayer:

God, have mercy upon me, a blind, ignorant, narrow-minded, pride-ridden, self-satisfied sinner; forgive me for not seeking after thy way and following it more closely; lead me now into the valley of thy presence where I can be still and learn the many lessons I have neglected; give me a clean heart, O God, and renew thy spirit within me and keep me ever awake and growing to the greatest possible likeness to Jesus Christ, thy Son, to whom I now dedicate anew my life.

The pin-down works in many different ways. It means never letting ourselves get away with anything that is not the truth. It means stripping ourselves of all camouflage and pretense, all intellectual and moral dishonesty. It means being and seeing what we are and, from this knowledge, erasing the untrue and the hastily sketched. All this on the plate of life we have been assigned to draw. We pin our souls down in order to ink-in heavily the lines and angles, carefully measured and in their true proportion, according to the standard Christian life-plan of Christ. When we get away with anything less than this, we are sinners in the sight of God, and the truth is not in us as a fully discovered possession.

We should never be afraid of the truth, for truth is God, and with him we are safe, for he is our Father — our best friend. His truth — himself indeed — will not ever let us down, but will lead us toward wholeness and completeness.

Now for demonstration number two. Have you ever been frightened when some guilt of yours has come close to being revealed, when you felt you were going to be pinned down to a confession? I have. Have you ever changed the subject abruptly when someone came too close to the truth which threatened to become an exposé of you? I have.

Peter was pinned down many times. "Whom do *ye* say that I am?" "This fellow is one of them." "Call no man unclean."

Peter later was able to declare, "We must obey God rather than men." He, too, made some decisions when pinned down.

But Judas refused to be pinned down. Let us look at Judas' type and see if we can put our finger on the significance of his example for our demonstration of the thumb-tacked soul. Judas represents a class of people who, though continually exposed to the good, the best, the highest, grow worse all the time instead of better. They seem to feel they have *arrived* and there is no more to say or do. They misunderstand the living, loving Christ and through their misunderstanding of him, betray him.

When we feel we have arrived and there is no more need for seeking the way and growing in it, we are complacent and are unwilling to be pinned down about our faith. Of course, it is our subconscious uncertainty about our faith which makes our resentment of being pinned down come so quickly to the surface. We are unwilling to be tested or to engage the enemy. We are not certain enough. We are not strong enough.

Many of you are familiar with the play "Lady in the Dark," which deals with the problem of a woman who was unwilling to compete as a woman, for fear she would be shown up by other feminine creatures. She became mentally tied up in knots. I have known of children who cried in a schoolroom because they were uncertain whether they could work the problem on the blackboard or not. A young midshipman was chosen because of ability and mental superiority to take a special advanced course. He refused on the grounds that he was afraid he might not make the grade.

Our minds seem to work like this. If we are never pinned down to an out-and-out showing up, no one will ever find us out, so we often reason. That is frequently one of the reasons why people do not come to the pastor's study when doubts assail and fears would destroy or to religious study courses and schools of religion, where more knowledge is available and old knowledge is checked; or are deaf to sermons because they do not want to hear, or feel they do not need to hear. If they were to do these things, they are afraid their souls would be thumbtacked and seen for what they are — skin-covered exhibitions of hypocrisy.

These people, who form a certain proportion of our church membership, are not only betraying Jesus, but themselves. They are missing the joy of abundant, free, loving life. This business of getting clear and keeping clear of soul-darkening blackness is hard, yes, but worth whatever is expended to gain it. The rewards are pretty automatic — sterile and dusty ones for those who refuse to submit to the thumbtacking technique; ever-increasing-in-wonder ones for those who are eager to get on a right basis and grow from there.

Jesus was willing to be pinned down. Note his experience in the wilderness — he had it out with his thumbtacked soul then before he began his ministry. Note his experience in the Garden of Gethsemane, before he completed his earthly ministry. He was pinned down to the choice made. It was the very nature of God's Son not to leave any loose ends flying.

There are many areas where this technique may be used to good advantage by all Christians.

Parents must be pinned down to their responsibilities to their children, especially adolescents; pinned down to where they will admit and assume this responsibility.

Christians are daily pinned down to their proper witness.

What disturbs people to a consciousness of difference as they watch us or listen to us? Is it Christ revealed and hunger for him aroused?

Carry away the technique and discover the area of your own need where it may be applied.

Where would this sermon lead us and what would it wish us to do, provided we accepted it and felt at least a bit of a need for it? To this point, along these lines of action: Who is going to run my life — God or me? Is there going to be any holding on to a single deviation from the life of Christ as we know it? For those of us who acknowledge we have been kidding ourselves and now want to end the play-acting, there is great joy in store.

For our summary and conclusion note well the following thoughts:

Examine your belief and ask and answer, " Is it real and vital? Does it dominate my life? Could I live without Christ? "

Am I ever sour?

Do I lack God's kind of outgoing love for others?

Am I so concerned with myself that Christ and others are pushed out and I grow stale in my little limited field?

Do I feel my brotherhood to all?

Do I think big thoughts or scrawny ones?

Our souls must be opened up all the way for God to see into every fold and crease and darkened cavern, and search out our real persons. Never be satisfied with your present power or size unless there is no longer any area where love and truth and expansion to a more Christly stature are needed. Keep this dialogue between Soul and Thumbtack confined to the concluding prayer form and remember the text: " You must be holy in *all* your conduct and conventions. Brace up your minds to get that holiness."

Dead Ends — Using Our Mistakes

"But we triumph even in our troubles, knowing that trouble produces endurance, endurance produces character, and character produces hope — a hope which never disappoints us, since God's love floods our hearts through the holy Spirit which has been given to us." (Romans 5:3-5)[1]

Paul means just what he says: Through Christ and his love for us we can glory in any tribulation and win victory over it through the power to endure and the hope that carries us through to the glory and the victory. Is this not good news? It is Paul's version of "Come unto me, all of you that are in the midst of trouble, and I will show you how to handle it." From the text and its meaning in brief part, we make a transition to the subject, "Dead Ends — Using Our Mistakes."

Wrong choices lead to mistakes; mistakes lead to dead ends; dead ends lead to troubles and frustrations, to the place where we are face to face with a closed door that apparently has no latch, no key. It is hard to keep hope alive, character intact, and endurance strong, at a dead end where we are used and ruled by our mistakes.

It is through ignorance or willful disobedience or accident that we reach our dead ends and are placed in a spot from which we emerge through Christ's open door, or in which we remain, to become controlled by circumstance and chalking up a frustrated, miserable existence to "fate."

God cannot erase the effects of our mistakes upon us and others, because he made us that way — free choosers of the way we would go. But we must remember that our choices are not always completely free at dead ends; they are conditioned by previously made decisions or by circumstance. For example, Christ on the cross could not choose to come

[1] From *The Bible, A New Translation*, by James Moffatt. Used by permission of Harper & Brothers.

down from the cross (because of a choice he had already
made to pay the cost of man's redemption), but he could
choose not to be bitter and unforgiving. We believe that
God can help us create something good from our mistakes,
under certain conditions of response to him and co-operation
with him. That is why Paul tells us to glory in our troubles,
because triumph is nigh; for they wake us up and make us
see and turn us around. God, through Christ — the loving
life and death of him — has provided an open door at every
dead end. Dead-enders will want to shout " Glory, Hallelujah " at this news. But wait, the latch on the door is on
the *inside*. It is really the door of our hearts, and the power
to open the door rests with the inner man — the conscious,
choosing power of each of us.

Glory in troubles? Certainly. It often takes the head-on
collision with some dead end to wake us up and make us
seek an open door. When we use suffering, adversity,
troubles of any kind, instead of being used by them, we
find that every dead end has a latch (inside us) and an
" openable " door. Blessed is the man who has troubles if
in them he finds God at last.

To dead-enders I would say hang on, and you will find
some of the secrets disclosed that will lead you to the latch-
string and the opening of the door. The way of the text
is the way we would follow.

Dead ends. The man adrift on a sea of sin; the man who
crouches alone in some dark corner; the woman whose love
cannot be requited; the blank wall men face when they come
to die; the man crumpled on the floor of some failure; the
birth that has made one a Jew or a Negro or a member of
a despised race; the man miserable in a job that tears his
heart and sears his mind and from which there is no visible
means of escape; the man who has been thwarted again and
again in his achievement of one thing after another; the man

consumed by fear that people will find out his secret sin;
the man who is reaching the breaking point in covering up
falsified accounts.

Dead ends all *until* God finds the opportunity to speak to
us, which he does *at every dead end when we stop to listen
for the sound of his voice and seek mayhap if we might find
him.* All we must do is to give up our self-worked-out
wisdom and turn humbly to God.

Paul was careful to explain that the triumph over distress
comes through our Lord Jesus Christ, who has provided a
way of access to the spirit of power — God's love in our
hearts. If God will answer through him our cries from the
despair of a dead end, we should turn for a moment to the
strategy of Jesus, who was God's love incarnate. He worked
wonders through his love for sinners, through his passionate
desire to transform them, bring them back, make them new
creatures. His love, inspired by God's life and light in
him, made him willing — yea, made him yearn — to take the
very refuse of our evil past and make a saint emerge from it,
as he did with Mary Magdalene.

Frank C. Laubach expresses it beautifully in *You Are My
Friends:* " Jesus has had an inveterate, incurable habit of
creating and transforming. Because it is his nature to change
bad to good, low to high, sorrow to joy, he loves us for
our need and our imperfections. He revels in making im-
perfection perfect. He loves us for our chains because his
joy is to break them. He loves us in prison because his joy
is to open prison doors. He loves us sick, because his joy is
to make us well. . . . Far greater than merely to make us well
or strong or peaceful or even happy. He aims at nothing
less than making us like him, so that we will possess all his
insatiable passion for lifting, healing, and transforming." [1]

[1] From *You Are My Friends,* by Frank C. Laubach. Harper & Brothers,
publishers. Used by permission.

Jesus can take the aching loneliness of one whose faith and love are lost in death and change the dead end of possessive love to the open door of expressive love — when we let him.

Jesus can take the pain of an incurable disease and use it as the raw material for fashioning something beautiful, useful, and fine, something beyond complaining, hurt feelings, blame, and resentment — when we deliberately set to work with him.

Jesus can take every loss and show us how to harvest it by never letting the good of the lost die in our hearts — when we are willing to look at our losses from the angle of the spiritual.

Jesus can take every destroyed community, ravaged by war, and declare the hope of reconstruction because God is in the midst of the ruins, mourning over the cruel results of man's wrong choices but issuing the command to build again and strengthen the foundations of the heart.

Jesus can take the habit of unkind gossip and help one to face the facts, accept them, and use them, and out of them bring tolerance and kindliness.

The point is, how? The dead-ender is impatient by now, if he has been in his condition long. Paul is our best example of one who never knew of dead ends, after the door opened in that first great brick wall. Oh, yes, we would call them dead ends — prison, suffering, shipwreck, failure, and the like — but not Paul. He gloried in his infirmities and tribulations, and triumphed over them, giving God the credit. Whatever he had and whatever he did is centered in Christ. "Nothing shall separate me from the love of God in Christ Jesus." How did it happen? How does it happen? In much the same way William of Sens changed a possible dead end into something useful. He caught an idle mason, as his chisel slipped and spoiled the saint he carved. William saw something could be made of what was yet left and, because of it, wrought out of the mistake a hippogriff, to help protect the cathedral against evil spirits. Dorothy L. Sayers tells the story in *The Zeal of Thy House*.[1]

The secret of Christ's door-opening power with men lies in the experience of the cross. Jesus, "The Man on the Cross," reminds passers-by that perhaps a cross does not matter so much after all, if one knows how to take it. No matter what our condition — physical or spiritual — Jesus will help us pass through the open door of faith, where we are so filled with his loving presence we are able to transcend the suffering of every present moment. "The Man on the Cross" can take all the bitterness, frustration, and resentment from our lives (that is what made the cross inevitable — the existence of man's bitterness, frustration, and resentment), and we too can in turn become open doors through which many will walk released, free from the prison-house of self. You see, even though Christ was crucified, the fact that he didn't allow bitterness and resentment to conquer him made the Crucifixion a victory.

In a story published recently of a modern Paul, who had reached the dead end of suffering and frustration, we read how he was brought to the point of simply turning toward the "Man on the Cross" when all else had failed, and how he found that just wanting him greatly brought order and peace to his thinking. This modern Paul, as he faced life squarely, seeking to see how he could use it to the utmost, often wondered if perhaps the basis of real prayer was not in this *preferring of God in every circumstance*. Because this became a belief, he read the life of Christ again and again, and what others said about him, drinking in every word hungrily. "As he read and longed and thought, mental

---

[1] From *The Zeal of Thy House*, by Dorothy L. Sayers. Harcourt, Brace and Company, Inc. Used by permission of Ann Watkins, Inc.

alertness and ingenuity flowed into him. Suggestions in-
complete at first, like words apart from sentences, assembled
in his mind. Slowly they took shape in complete ideas,
clarifying his initiative and heightening his energies." [1] This
is the way he discerned God's plan for him at a dead end.
This is the way he found the latch, opened the door and
stepped through. By just letting go of the resentments
which had sapped his vitality, he became a new and free
creature, no longer chained at a dead end.

Jesus said that in the world we would have tribulation,
because he knew that some men would remain ignorant and
careless and unconcerned about anyone but self; that these
would choose unwisely and foolishly and bring judgment
upon innocent and guilty alike in a world built upon laws
which must be obeyed if they are not to work against us.
But he added, "Be of good cheer, I have overcome the
world." That is, by the technique of giving wholehearted
attention to discovering God's laws, his will, and his way,
we can rise above and be happy in spite of evil circumstance.
Jesus said, "I am the door." We could add with surety this
word: "Look at God through my eyes, think about God
through my mind. He will reveal the way we must walk,
at least a step at a time, as fast as we can travel."

Here are the steps to take if we find ourselves dead-enders:

First we must stop trying to do everything on our own.
We must bring God into the picture and in his presence
turn loose all the powers of light with which he has endowed
us. This process will reveal self in its true condition. Bringing God into the picture will give an objective calmness that
makes sense out of hopelessness. This will shift our thinking
from negative to positive and our concern from self at the
center to self in relation to the whole. We shall be honest

[1] From *The Open Door*, by Floyd Van Keuren. Harper & Brothers,
publishers. Used by permission.

if we keep the vision of Christ near enough to compare ourselves with him. This is first. Take stock in order to gain height. Perspective will lead to the vision of the whole, and outlets will begin to appear.

Second. Once we have willingly faced the facts of the situation in the presence of God, and turned all the powers of mind and heart loose upon them, we catch a glimpse of what we can be — should be already, if we have begun to live under the guiding sense of God's presence and the constant illumination of his spirit. We begin to relate the facts to at least the little we are sure of and truly believe, and our action pattern begins to shape up. We are gradually discerning some of the things that must be done.

Third. We carry through step by step the plan of action which has evolved and bear in mind Paul's words about glory and triumph and hope. This, with the cross, should move us through the open door of decision into a new and more wonderful world.

Fourth. Read books which may help.[1] The steps revealed are clues for us to follow. Talk with doctor, minister, loved one or friend, who will be trustworthy, whom you respect and admire, who will keep you moving toward the freedom of your highest. Never give up — never let down. It may take a long time. But character and endurance and hope will be present because of Christ's love flooding our repentant and released hearts.

[1] *Release,* by Starr Daily. Harper & Brothers, New York. *You Are My Friends,* by Frank C. Laubach. Harper & Brothers, New York. *Haven House,* by James W. Kennedy. John Knox Press, Richmond, Virginia.

CHAPTER II

SERMONS FOR SPECIAL OCCASIONS

And ye are witnesses of these things.
LUKE 24:48

SOME of the advantages which come from writing out sermons verbatim are: easily made copies for those who request them; an opportunity for offering especially good ones for publication in a denominational magazine, or for issuing in pamphlet form, or for printing excerpts in the weekly bulletin; also a file copy which is polished and ready for use again as the need arises. But remember, a sermon is a sermon and should not be disguised as an article or a talk or a radio address. It will always be recognized for what it is.

A preacher should not read from published sermons with the general purpose of gaining an outline and the material for his own next preaching engagement, but rather for inspiration, new ideas, and for opening up undreamed-of avenues of approach to his people.

For special occasions and for the treatment of particular themes, sermons of others should be read in order to find clues to one's own plan for presenting a message vital and different enough to catch ears, hold minds and compel lives. I have selected a sermon for Race Relations Sunday to illustrate a special occasion.

We Are Our Brother's Brother

If color is the unfinished business of democracy, we should roll up our sleeves and be about finishing it. There is no question before us today that is thornier or more perplexing.

But we are faced with the facts of it, and, as Christians, we cannot refuse to come to grips with them.

If the Jewish problem makes the New Yorker's blood curdle; if the Oriental question makes the Californian see red; if the Mexican question arouses the ire of the border Texan; if the many foreign born residing in our large northern cities make the natives writhe with resentment; if the Indian is the bugbear of the midwesterner; and if the question of Negro " rights " makes the Southerner boil, I should say we have some clear indications of a race problem in America. Because of the openly bitter antagonisms sharply before us, the grave need is evident; and our responsibility for dealing with it as far as we are able cannot be denied.

Unless we as Christians can discuss the question without the hot passion that blinds us; and unless we can work out, enunciate, and stand by a statement of principle declaring equal concern and opportunity for all peoples (which means all patronage must go), we might as well quit the struggle for freedom and permanent peace, for it will never be attained.

We are very sympathetic, as a rule, with the plight of racial minorities and their difficulties under persecution in Europe and elsewhere, but when we come to our own land, in our own home town, things are " different." Hypocrites we are unless we help to make good the church's age-old theme: " Christ for the *world* we sing." By which we mean: Love must emerge as constructive good will and an honest concern for the welfare of others. Our Christian love must overcome the background of fear that our special privileges will be taken away. Those who build up ill will and resentment of a minority race by their attitude of patronage and superiority, only add fuel to the fire by which their children will be burned. Far-sighted Christian people will be busy about building up good will — genuine, loving concern.

We must never forget that race prejudice is a disease. It has not yet been made non-infectious, but I believe the remedy for it, wherever it is found, to be essential Christianity: namely, the belief that God is the Father of all, that all men are his sons and our brothers and must be treated with dignity and respect; and that in Jesus Christ there cannot be any discrimination based upon race, or upon any other human misconception of rights and privilege.

The best story for giving us a lead about what to do in this dilemma is Peter's vision and his dealing with Cornelius, a Gentile, in the book of Acts. The story in brief: Cornelius, a devout Greek captain of Caesarea, had a vision. An angel told him to send messengers to one Peter in Joppa. Peter, at the noon hour and just before the messengers arrived, was praying on the roof top, and he was very hungry. He too had a vision — of ceremonially clean and unclean food. A voice told him to eat, that God had made it all clean. This happened three times. Then the messengers from Cornelius arrived. Peter heard them out. He went with them to Cornelius, taught them of Christ, converted and baptized the entire household, and learned his greatest lesson, that no man is unimportant to God.

It took more than a decade to free the disciples from this ancient race prejudice against the Gentiles and to bring them to the point of following Christ's way. Jesus had tried to break down this prejudice by word and deed. His final words on earth were, " Go ye into all the world and preach the gospel to *every* creature." But Peter's mind was still paralyzed by custom, which was more important to him and all the Jews than a fresh revelation of God's truth. That is, it was more important until this vision came, when Peter, no doubt inspired by these remembered teachings of Christ, overcame this block to his ministry. As Peter meditated on this vision, the Holy Spirit spoke to him — the Holy Spirit speaks sometimes when we face a problem with all our thoughts, with all of our powers of concentration and none of our prides — and he knew what to do and he did it. " God has taught me not to call any one vulgar or unclean. . . . Now I really understand that God shows no partiality, but welcomes the man of any nation who reveres him and does what is right. . . . He is Lord of us all." (Acts 10:28; 34-36)[1] The light had come for Peter at last.

However, the Church in Jerusalem, hearing with amazement of Peter's conduct, summoned him there to explain his actions. He did so, concluding his report with these words, " Who was I that I could withstand God? " And all who heard were persuaded. But Peter had been willing to follow the vision; to re-examine his prejudices in the light of God's Holy Spirit. Result: the disciples were convinced and the universal catholic character of Christianity began to make conquest of the world. Peter realized at long last that we are our *brother's brother* and that a Christian's mind is *covetous for God's truth which he desires to share with all*.

This story gives some insight into the method of dealing with the race problem today, how to live up to our highest light even when we are under social pressure.

Since the racial predicament in most communities is largely confined to the Negro, we shall deal specifically with that conundrum. But I beg of you not to close your minds and simply realign your prejudices. Let us think together on this vital problem which must be in the process of solution if we are to win the peace now that the war has ended, and if we are to lay strong foundations for a real Christian world community. We face the quandary then, as Christians, with fair-minded objectiveness. (And I urge this with special

[1] From *The Bible, An American Translation*, by Smith and Goodspeed. Used by permission of the University of Chicago Press.

emphasis upon youth, who will carry the problem in their hearts much nearer to the point of final solution.)

If we read the Declaration of Independence and the Bill of Rights and the Constitutional Amendment which frees slaves and recognizes them as human beings instead of chattel, we would think them free and equal citizens of this country. But when we study the laws and customs, and the attitudes of some leaders in the South, who talk about white supremacy and disprove it by example at the same time, we find that the right of franchise is restricted, men are denied access to the polls, and bill after bill seeking to guarantee these constitutional rights is defeated by Congress. The basic assumptions lying back of all these discriminatory and finally indefensible acts as stated by a recent writer are: " the inequality of races, the inherent right of one race to enjoy privileges denied another race, the right of one race to stand on the neck of another race." [1] These are totally wrong assumptions, as has been demonstrated to all who are willing to see and learn.

There are two groups among the Negroes working on this baffling problem. There are those who want to fight ahead now, regardless of what will happen; and there are also those who are willing to take more time in a co-operative process. This latter group will win more quickly and constructively, I believe, if not balked by well-meaning people, by well-meaning church people. A meeting several years ago in Durham, North Carolina, of just such a group of substantial responsible southern Negroes, gives us great hope of racial understanding and harmony. Their statement of aims is sane, without malice or ill will, and it has brought a vast amount of positive approval from Southerners, both white and black. Since then, the forming of state and local

[1] From *On Final Ground*, by Harold A. Bosley. Harper & Brothers, publishers. Used by permission.

interracial commissions has gone on rapidly and the progress is evident in the new tolerance and understanding between the races living in these areas. The war hastened the process. It will depend largely upon our intelligent handling of the problem and our Christianizing of it as to which group wins out eventually. The former one would win through forcing issues and arousing strife; the other would win through the God-given power of patient and forgiving understanding, and interracial co-operation. This we must further now at all costs, by working with them. If we refuse to help this latter group, we shall be inadvertently placing fuel on the fire started by the former.

As I watched the steel framework of a new building going up under my hotel window all of one month, I thought how slowly it took form. But the more I pondered, the better I understood how much more solid and strong the building would be with such an inner strength to back up its outer beauty and usefulness. So with our bonds of racial under-standing — riveted together slowly, under the enduring process of Christian love.

Every person who declares for Christ must do these things *now:*

(1) Take seriously — really *believing* — the words of Peter in our text that " God is Lord of all."

(2) Seek solutions intelligently, with tolerance, without blindness of group prejudice. This involves getting all the facts from every angle and putting them together objectively and in the light of our belief. There are many sources. Every periodical of social and international concern deals with the race problem in some manner in almost every issue.

(3) Recognize a few basic aims and stand by them, such as the things we have avowedly been fighting for recently at *such a cost:* Equal opportunity of freedom for all peoples; no discrimination and no prejudice.

These Christian attitudes and convictions have been re-
inforced by a statement from the Federal Council of
Churches of Christ in America, converging on one conclusion: Man must be treated as man, apart from race, birth,
and color, as part of God's great family on earth. As proof
of this possibility the message declares: Science agrees that
the blood of humanity is one; that there are no permanently
inferior or superior races, although innate capacities vary
somewhat. Its basic principle is equality of opportunity for
all. That " all " must mean *all* or it means nothing. There
are no exceptions. These words are still emblazoned on the
Liberty Bell — " Proclaim liberty throughout all the land
unto all the inhabitants thereof." (Leviticus 25:10)

There are three common erroneous views, which are attempts to rationalize racial attitudes, both in the North and
in the South. The phrase "social equality" explains one
attitude. Another worn-out cliché is that "intermarriage
is inevitable." These ideas are bugaboos, smoke screens,
which someone is always ready to throw around any dis-
cussion of this question in order to obscure the real issue,
the real issue being Christian brotherhood and respect for
persons. From the experiences in other places where intermarriage is permissible, we find very little intermingling
with any disparate groups. This is not a present problem
in America.

Another widespread attitude and belief, although it has
been disproved scientifically, is that the Negro race is inherently inferior and racially about where it belongs. This
is where Schickelgruber stood, and all who believe it still
stand with him. He revealed the ghastly disease of race
prejudice in its most advanced stage. What is the record
of that for history?

All of these attitudes produce inner tensions and fears
which make for sensitiveness and touchiness. The resolution

of these fears and tensions by Christian relaxation, which comes from belief in God and his loving concern and equal care for all his children, will do much to clear the air.

God said to Peter, God tells us, that we shall call no man common or unclean . . . who reveres him and does what is right.

Racial prejudice is a left-over from our savage days and the existence of it in a land dedicated to the proposition that all men are created equal is distinctly out of place. If " in God we trust," then treat all men as brothers we must.

As Christians we must face the riddle of this distraction, for we are up to our necks in it, and we must accept and stand by the basic principles already enunciated, applying them *alike* and *always* to every *if* and *but*.

We must sacrifice our race prejudice or freedom will not ring except from a cracked bell of liberty, whose sound is feeble and hardly heard at all. Certainly such ringing will not be heard " throughout all the land, unto all the inhabitants thereof."

If you have listened to this sermon with an open mind and a calmly beating heart, I know there is hope. We cannot do it all overnight, of course. We shall make mistakes. And we do not want to over-simplify. We cannot issue a blank check to any group, but we can have a right inner attitude toward them and they toward others, and keep everyone pushing toward sonship. We must recognize the fact that people who have long been exploited often seek to repay in kind when their powers increase. There will be unwise leadership; the conduct of leaders both white and black will not always be Christian, honest, and scrupulous. But this must not be an excuse for us to use in failing to come to the rescue of society endangered by this bomb, with a short fuse already lit and sputtering. The question demands of Christians much humility, patience, and magnanimity.

This much is clear: we *must* do what we can do, and I believe we can make a stand on the principles already mentioned of equality of opportunity and no discrimination, an unyielding respect for justice and rights under law — God's law and man's — for all men. But only the individual soul can get rid of its prejudices. Therefore, we must seek daily through God's help to surrender our own race prejudice by concentrating on the good in the race we look down upon, seeing them as individuals and not as a mass of color. We must test the rate and extent of their present progress and condition with our own as to the distance they and we are from our respective primitive states.

Remember: " He who has less of Christ than I is my inferior; he who has the same amount of Christ as I is my equal; and he who has more of Christ than I is my superior."

Peter had a vision and was convinced; he followed the leading of the vision and significant things happened to a family and the entire Christian fellowship. We too must catch just such a convincing vision and act upon it. What God has created is *not* unclean. Therefore we can call *no* man common. We must acknowledge as spiritual brothers all who revere the Father and abide by his laws, and all others as potential sons of God. We must keep fighting to maintain Christ as Lord of us all, with the belief that the world will yet be free of race prejudice and that human brotherhood will grow into the kingdom of God on earth. " Something more is expected of us, as followers of Jesus Christ — and, God willing, we shall not fail."

O God of all who dwell on the face of the whole earth, help us to see the light of Christ coming into the world through many colored windows, and help us to blend it and give to all life the atmosphere of thy kingdom, the reality of thy eternal Spirit presence among us; and dear Father, make us all able to understand and follow thy teaching that we are in truth our brother's brother. Amen.

*   *   *

Sometimes, when the service is quite long, the weather is hot, or the service of Holy Communion is held, a short sermonette will be more appropriate than a sermon. I append a selection with a great variety of themes to show the possibilities of a fairly brief, compact, sermonic utterance.

Living Epistles

Brethren, I declare unto you the gospel which I preached unto you, which also ye have received, and wherein ye stand; by which also ye are saved, if ye keep in memory what I preached unto you, unless ye have believed in vain.

1 Corinthians 15:1, 2

On the golf course there is used frequently a descriptive phrase after one misses the ball, slices, hooks, or tops it: " I don't know why I did that." But we do know why. It is because we did not choose to practice, to take a lesson, to remember to keep our heads down, our eyes on the ball, or to follow through.

The same is true of repeated moral failure. We say: " I don't know why I did that," or " I don't know what made me do that." But we do. We did not choose to remember, to practice, or to consider results. We keep right on repeating our mistakes, thinking we'll get away with them this time, surely. But cause and effect follow one another relentlessly, in spiritual law as well as in natural law. There is no escape from the result of our choices when we disobey that law. Conscience was made to enable us to make right choices based upon knowledge of the ends. Only man has this ability.

The reasons why we are not better golfers and better men

is because we choose to make our choices different from what they should be; we do not expend the time and effort necessary for overcoming our weaknesses.

The text is just as applicable today as it was to the Christian church in Corinth. The need is for us to think on a few of its implications.

Paul found the church people of Corinth in the same trouble as the golfer who has learned and forgotten, or who has never learned. They had received the gospel — Paul repeats what he taught them about Christ. They had been presumably saved by it — identified and committed to the teaching and the person of Christ. They were supposed to be standing strong on their beliefs, living by them, even as all professing Christians.

But Paul finally intimates that some have forgotten the gospel, the means of their salvation, have forgotten about Jesus Christ; or else they had never really believed in him and accepted him in the first place, in which event their conversion had been a sham. Even as church members only.

One of the instruments Jesus left for helping us to determine our right choices is the service of Holy Communion. So that we could " keep in memory," so that we might not have " believed in vain." Note the number of times the word " remembrance " is used in the service.

It takes practice to learn the art of living as well as of golfing. There are few if any irremedial reasons for duffer golf or muffed lives. God's laws are never changeable. Do this and that will result. Even the laws of golf are like this. The great sin of modern America is that we think we can separate cause from effect, that we can eat our cake and have it too; that, somehow, God's law does not apply to us, today.

What does it all add up to?

That we must strive to keep in remembrance our beliefs

(given us by Jesus Christ to rule our lives) until the habit of living by them has been established; to come near, to hear about him, to worship him, and to give him thanks, even as now. For the golfer it is: relax, head down, eye on ball, follow through. For the Christian it is: relax in faith — God is dependable, trustworthy; head down in humility — lean upon him for strength and guidance; eyes on Christ — never let him out of your mind's eye — " looking to Jesus 'til glory doth shine," and follow through with acts accordingly.

That is the summary of the Epistle for today: our lives must be living epistles, which can be and are read by all men, men who can tell by their reading who it is we worship and serve.

Good-by, God

On this hot July morning, with the sound of firecrackers still popping in our ears and with thoughts of vacation time dancing in our heads, I am reminded of the story of the little girl who said in her prayers one summer morning: " Good-by, God, today we are all going on our vacation."

That story speaks volumes of truth, for about this time of year a general condition of spiritual lethargy descends upon Christians. Cabins are opened or rented, sun suits or swim suits are donned, hammocks swing gently with their heavy burdens, and the paraphernalia of vacation time makes its appearance in everything from fishing rods to mosquito lotion.

Don't misunderstand me. We should be thinking such thoughts. Vacations are needed and are helpful for the best interests of life. But not divorced from spiritual things. Not good-by, God; hello, beach or mountain or grandpa's farm. We don't leave our souls at home in a dark closet just because we expose our bodies to the sun and insects.

Man is not a number of sections to be dismembered at

will. He is a whole, a oneness, and no part of him can exist healthily separated from any other part or separated from God.

In the setting of this service of remembrance, a few thoughts may help to center us on realities, and help to free us from the temptation to say the little girl's prayer.

Note the words of Luke's Gospel: " Go after that which is lost " and " joy over one sinner that repenteth." The most fruitful period of spiritual growing and power is vacation time, when people are together in leisurely fashion, when the tempo of living has slowed down, when there is quietness, when God seems much closer as his creation surrounds us.

Instead of a time of temptation, of pulling us away from God, our vacations can be a time of catching up and passing on what we know of God.

Strange as it may seem, it is still necessary to introduce God to the world. Especially to those who have said, " Good-by, God; hello, science; hello, education; hello, reason." We've seen the results of man trying to administer God's world while he leaves God out. Not Good-by, God; but Come, God, help us show man the missing element in his life and in the life of the world at large, that he may learn there can be no world without thee.

Our job is to keep the faith, even though others do not; to talk about God, that we may settle our beliefs as well as pass truth and light along to others. Our summer conversations should keep God and what we know of his plans for the world to the fore, whether atomic power or the starving in Europe be the theme. If questions come which are too much for us, we must dig for answers.

All through this service of remembrance comes the admonition to seek the lost ones. " When thou art converted, strengthen the brethren." The spiritual element is not a ghostly fog to grasp at, but a divine imperative to live life to the full.

In the war against materialism and secularism where everybody is for himself, there can be no letdown, no rest, no coasting. It can never be vacation time from spiritual things if we would keep the world alive, if we would influence and guide men to the right use of knowledge and power. The world's awry and ripe for repentance. We who know Him, even a little, must talk about Him and His way for us, as shown through Jesus Christ, and live according to our faith.

Never "Good-by, God, today we are all going on a vacation," but rather "God helping me, I will do my best with what I have, so far as I can, where I am each day, for Jesus Christ."

Frustrating God's Miracle

These are they which came out of great tribulation, and have washed their robes, and made them white in the blood of the Lamb. Therefore are they before the throne of God, and serve him day and night in his temple: and he that sitteth on the throne shall dwell among them.

Revelation 7:14, 15

There are two sides to Holy Scripture.

One, like all other writings, is simply that it is a medium of communication which calls for the same mutuality of understanding, the same immediacy of experience, and the same self-activity which men ordinarily give to any writing. This is the outward and visible.

The second, unlike most other writings, is the inner secret revealed of the outer radiance manifest; the power to lift one out of his earth-bound experience into the pure light of God, where he may behold himself, the true shape of his destiny, and what by the grace of God in Christ he may become. This is the inward and spiritual.

The outward and visible part of our text. Great creative literature that speaks to men's hunger for the eventual answer to sorrow and all other travail of soul. The glory of the passage would be destroyed by analysis. The author begins with a description of God's care for the Jewish Christians, but his ecstasy from the vision he gains, while meditating on God's care, carries him beyond the limits of Israel and the first century.

The inward and spiritual part. A new understanding and insight into the blessedness which awaits those who trust in God. They will *come out* of their time of suffering, washed clean of their pain and bitterness, their loneliness and sense of frustration and loss; they will worship God forever because he has enabled them to live when they wanted to die, to go on when they wanted to give up.

When we refuse such insights, to go beyond the present or the visible, we are frustrating God's miracle of life never ending and of blessings never failing.

God's words work miracles when heard and heeded.

An Introductory Good Friday Address

No corner of the world is immune to the manifestation of immortality. This came to me the other evening, as I listened to a symphony written by a Russian. I knew that here was evidence of the kind of life for which man was created. The music, indeed a lament for the world dying and a solemn requiem for its ebbing life, filled me for a moment with an aching, not of despair exactly nor of sorrow, but of silence, ominous and heavy. In the dying strains of the vast depths of the finale, in the heavy prolonged quietness, my inward self, though drained and filled again by turns, began to flow with a conviction of hope. The very music itself became the reason why the life of man's best could never die, and became the soul-stirring promise of a world to be after tragedy's little hour. The tragedy of this hour in time is not the end of an era in death and destruction, but that man, capable of such an experience as the creation of an immortal symphony, must sleep so long and wake so late in the midst of ashes and ruins. Only as man is brought low in the midst of his self-sufficiency will the greater life of identification with the upbuilding, heaven-bringing processes of God's way be seen and possessed.

Even though we are witnessing, literally, the crucifixion of a world, and are mourning for it; and even though something dies in us daily as we read the story of its agony, we cannot still the rising tide of understanding concerning another crucifixion, the dying of a man of love on a dead tree.

As we grow strangely quiet and relaxed within today in the presence of this fact, and as we tread lightly before witnessing the death which has come to a man and is coming to men, we see *light* in the darkness and *life* on the cross; and through it all power seems to loom, begging to be taken and used; power to overcome that which brings death to a man, to men; the power to become a deathless son of God, an eternal witness to his creative way of love. For God does not deal in endings and in death. That which is of him in us, the best and highest of which we are capable, will never see an end save of evil, but will be part of an everlasting beginning. If a Russian has produced a symphony such as the one I heard the other night, and through it has given me a message which transcends time and language and bloody tragedy, then God's way is possible in every corner of the earth, in the heart of every man; and the hope of brotherhood stirs without ceasing in the treetops of our age, as the wind of God blows past.

We must remember that death is never an end to life but only a change in life; that life is of God and cannot end, only change. The slow death of the world today is due to sin — man's choice of the lesser, evil way. The death we are witnessing is in reality, then, the death of self caused by sin, for evil feeds upon its very self and destroys itself. This makes the world's tragedy a lonely tragedy of the un-repenting human soul. When we see the cross of Jesus and watch him dying there, we know the results of all sin — and we fall upon our knees in remorse for our share in it. *We* are the crucifiers of a world until *we* die unto sin and rise unto the newness of a life which places God's Christ at the center.

As this miracle of redemption is repeated in a thousand hearts, the death-rattle of the world will cease and in its place will be heard the faint strains of a joy-song that will rebuild the waste places with every known evil left out. And so we come today to find life in a death, and we shall so find.

* * *

A few things to keep in mind when writing or preparing sermons short or long:

Writing sermons out completely lends exactness and cor-rectness of utterance. But reading sermons verbatim from the pulpit usually bores the listener. Vary the pattern and keep free from a stereotyped approach every time. To be one-self (all of oneself) is the beginning of effective preaching. Never let the bare bones of sermonic structure dance about in public without the flesh of content and purpose, nor allow the personality of the preacher to obscure Christ.

Oliver Wendell Holmes had his say on almost every sub-ject, as we discover upon reading *The Autocrat of the Break-fast Table*. Sermons and preachers did not escape his notice. This chapter might well end with his pointed remark for our pondering:

" Most decent people hear one hundred lectures or sermons on theology every year — and this, twenty, thirty, fifty years together. . . . The clergy, however, rarely hear any sermons except what they preach themselves. A dull preacher might be conceived, therefore, to lapse into a state of quasi-heathenism, simply for the want of religious instruction." [1]

Sermons must be windows opening in order to let in God's light, God's truth and the freshness of his Spirit. And they must let these things into the lives of preacher and listener as well.

[1] From *The Pastor*. The Methodist Publishing House. Used by permission.

CHAPTER III

EVERYONE LIKES A STORY

My tongue is the pen of a ready writer.
PSALMS 45:1

MANY of us are duds when talking to children, usually speaking far beyond their understanding, and being unable to translate our message to their level of comprehension. The made-up story is always arresting, if it is good, and every child of almost every age responds immediately to whatever is clothed in " Once upon a time." With a little practice in telling and writing more exactly, we can gain ease and facility in producing children's stories as the occasion demands. Seldom can we put our hands on a good story which fits. Who cares! Make one up. I remember the church-school picnic when it rained and I was forced to tell a story. An old desire to know why the larkspur has a rabbit face came to mind, and I launched forth and carried on to a highly improbable conclusion. But the story saved the day. It cured my fear of trying such things and gave me the courage to tell stories with more religious point to them.

The educators have locked horns upon the value of tacking morals onto stories. But I agree with the conclusions of Dr. Ernest M. Ligon of Union College, Schenectady, New York, famed pioneer in character research from the religious point of view, when he says his experiments indicate that unless a specific moral is tacked on, the child will not only not get the point, but will usually get an entirely wrong one.

Strive for simplicity; keep characters and incidents close to the child's experience, and don't be afraid to gesture and pantomime. Children have vivid imaginations. You can even draw a picture or map on the air in front of them and they can actually see it there. An excellent device for maintaining interest over several days, such as during a daily vacation Bible school, is to tell the stories in thriller serial style — getting to an exciting moment at the end of each installment and not resolving the situation until next time.

A ready story-telling technique will stand the clergyman in good stead at many needy moments of his ministry.

The best way to develop the story-telling habit is to try making up originals when one's own children call for a story. Almost any theme will do. Even the animal kingdom and the flower kingdom can be brought to life and filled with meaning. I know *Alice in Wonderland* is for adults but the idea at first grew from a story made for a child. I know also that such modern books as *Rumor in the Forest* were written for mature minds. But when the medium, be it allegory or fairy tale, reaffirms Christlike love, it has pointed the way to fulfill Christ's admonition: "Forbid them not; for of such is the kingdom of heaven."

The Little Tree That Wouldn't Grow

In a beautiful forest of fir trees there once grew a patch of seedlings. These little treelings were just beginning to feel their growing pains sharpen within. It made them proud, and all of them were determined to grow as big and beautiful as their near-by parents. That is, all but one little tree. He was very lazy and reasoned like this: If I stay small, my brother and sister trees will grow up around me and their branches will grow strong and large and protect me from the bitter winds of winter and the heavy clinging snow, and the dreaded woodman's ax. The little tree thought he was very smart and would not listen to the warning of the older trees to grow and grow and grow. So he closed his eyes tight against the sun, and his mouth against the sweet-smelling air; he refused to breathe in the warmth of spring and summer, and his roots he held away from the little pools of water beneath the ground. And the little tree remained stubby (short for stubborn) while the other trees grew taller and taller, stronger and stronger, and more beautiful. But the little tree smiled to himself and lazed along, refusing to grow.

One winter, as the little tree was asleep and snug, protected from the winds and the snow, sounds of chopping rang through the forest. The axman had come for the annual Christmas tree-cutting. But the little tree did not worry, even though shortly his brother and sister trees were chopped down all around him. He was ignored. After the axman had hauled the trees away, though, the little tree who wouldn't grow began to shake and shiver. He hadn't thought of this. No longer were strong branches over him and around him to protect him. The wind howled and almost tore off his slender weak branches; the snow piled high and threatened to break him in two. He was all alone and miserable. He wished again and again he had grown with the rest. They would soon be the center of some joyful home, warm and loved. But he was not good for anything. He was sad and sorry he hadn't grown. And he vowed in his heart to mend his ways with the coming spring and to grow just as fast as ever he could. But until then, the long dreary winter stretched before him; and he hugged to himself his scrawny little branches and settled down to getting through the winter as best he could, all alone against the cold.

But the week before Christmas brought two experiences. One which saddened; one which gladdened.

One night as he shook miserably, he heard music coming from a country church high on a neighboring hill. He could just make out the words repeated over and over by many voices, "no never, no never; not ever, not ever." The poor repentant little tree thought this meant he would never be able to grow again. And this made him very, very sad.

But on Christmas Eve he heard a lonely footfall or two in the silent forest and soon discovered a young lad with an ax, looking for a beautiful tree. But he couldn't find a pretty one and was nearly weeping. The little tree was terribly sorry for the little boy; indeed, he wished some miracle could happen to make him *just* the kind of tree the little boy wanted.

The tree whispered, "Little boy, little boy, come over here and cut me down."

"Oh, you're too small," the boy replied. Then he looked thoughtful. "But since you're the biggest and best one left, I guess I'll have to take you."

So he cut down the tree and carried it home.

It was warm in the cozy little home, with a cheery fire and three small children. They did the best they could with decorations on his frail limbs; then all went to bed. The house grew quiet and the little tree began to think. And he thought he heard sounds of singing. He had often heard the stars and the wind singing in the forest. This song sounded strangely like the one from the church a few nights before, but the words were different. The sound came, and the words "forever, forever; yes ever, yes ever." Could it be the stars were trying to tell him it was never too late to grow? A wild joy possessed him and he felt new life surging within him. Now must be the time; the spring would never come for him again. Since he could not now get his wish for another chance to take in the sun and the rain, he must do the best he could with this night. He opened his eyes wide and drew in the light from the fire, he breathed deep of the warmth of the room; the moisture of the atmosphere seeped into him and he began to grow. It was not too late for him to grow. And he grew and grew and grew all through the night.

The next morning, bright and early, the children came bouncing into the room ready to shout Merry Christmas! But they stopped and were silent. The tree — what had happened! Little Susan, age six, squeaked, " O Mommy, God worked a miracle and made it beautiful." And the little tree was so happy the tips of its needly fir twinkled and danced and he knew now that he should have grown straight and tall and beautiful as God had intended from the beginning. And he longed to tell everyone the great truth he had learned: We were born to grow and do something useful in the world; and it is never, never, too late!

The Poor Penny

There was once a penny who was very sad because he couldn't buy much and was despised by each owner he had. He was often given away or lost in the dirt. And even when a child's hand picked him up he was good for only one piece of candy. He cried often. His tears mingled with the grime of pockets and the places where he often fell, and he got dirtier and dirtier, sadder and sadder.

One day, after lying in a crack of a sidewalk for a long time, he was found by a child and carefully picked up and put in her pocket. "Soon another gumdrop, I suppose," he said to himself. But no, after the little girl got home he heard a different speech. Instead of " one gumdrop, please," he heard a prayer which ended with " You are God's children." The little girl then squeezed him into a dark box with a lot of other pennies who seemed very happy. He asked them what they were doing there. One of them, a very bright penny, replied, " We are being saved. We are no longer just copper pennies. We are God's children and in his sight are worth as much as nickel, or silver, or gold." The poor penny thought and thought on these words. At last he realized part of what had happened. He was going to be used for something quite wonderful, something to do with God's word and God's work.

The days passed quickly. Sometimes the little girl would pick up the box and rattle the pennies together. They didn't mind at all.

Then one day the poor penny heard singing and an organ playing. Right after this the box was torn open and the pennies were dumped into a pile of other pennies and nickels and dimes and even a few quarters. Some people counted them in great excitement and put them into bags. Then followed much journeying by train. The pennies were divided again and again, but each new group of penny friends told the poor penny the same story — " great things are in store for us." The hardest part was the waiting and the long times of traveling. But at last he found himself at rest on a hard table in a warm quiet place. Someone was untying the money bag, excitedly. As the poor penny slid out with his many brothers, he saw the big eyes of a little child. He had never seen a child like this before. It was a little boy with slanting eyes, yellow skin, and black hair. The child was in bed. It was a hospital bed. Then the poor penny knew this was the great thing God was sending them to do. So he spoke to the child, " You are God's child." The big eyes filled with light and joy. " My friends and I have come to make you well."

The poor penny no longer felt unimportant and alone, for he was carrying God's word and helping to do God's work.

His message is our message to the world: "All of you are God's children and our brothers and sisters whom we love."

I Wonder

Do you know where fairies and brownies live? (Tap head.) Right here in our minds. They represent our beautiful deeds and good desires. In our imaginations we see them busy at their work, happy and in a hurry, and we love them — the little people of our own creation. Now I want to tell you something like a fairy story today. Forget whatever else you may be thinking about and fill your mind with these words from a famous poem: " Twinkle, twinkle, little star. How I wonder. . . ."

Did you know that only stars twinkle? Planets never do. Notice the next time the stars are out. Some twinkle, some do not. The twinkly spots of light are stars, which God created for his vast universe. How many of you can wink? Some of you still have to learn to wink just one eye at a time. The stars had to learn and it took them a long time. But they do it very well now. Don't you think?

Once upon a time, a little boy was reciting the poem " Twinkle, twinkle, little star," lying on his back in the grass on a summer evening. All of a sudden he stopped at the end of these words, " How I wonder." In his mind he thought, " Why do the stars twinkle? " He tried to imagine, but couldn't. That night he had a dream.

He dreamed he awoke and through the ceiling of his room he saw a star winking at him as if to say, " Come on up." It seemed to pull him right out of bed and up through the ceiling, sailing toward the star. It got brighter and brighter the closer he came. At last he landed gently in a most beautiful city, where everything was sparkling bright and all the people were happy-looking. There were all sorts of little boys and girls running and playing and laughing. He stopped one of the boys and asked why the star twinkled so when seen from earth. The little boy took him by the hand and led him to a large balcony that seemed to hang out between all the stars.

"Look at the earth," he said.

There, far below, was a little ball just like any other planet.

The little star boy continued. "See, there is no winking there now, but soon it will shine even brighter than our starland. But this happens just once a year. A long time ago even the stars did not shine. Then a baby was born and God lighted each star to welcome the little baby boy. The stars have never ceased to twinkle, for they are still so happy that God sent the little baby to help make men better. The stars remind the people of earth every night of God's love for them in sending a baby who grew to be a man — the Lord Jesus."

The little boy awoke from his beautiful dream. He ran outside. There were the stars, millions of them twinkling with happiness because Jesus was born among men.

We are thankful and happy for the twinkly stars which remind us of Jesus Christ.

That's our fairy tale.

Perhaps we can remember that Jesus is within us and, although we can't be stars actually, we can help brighten the world because of him wherever we are. We can make our eyes into stars which shine with love for him and for all his children everywhere. Remember to give light from your star within every day.

The Sweet Peas' Tiny Hands

Once upon a time two little sweet-pea seeds nestled snugly together in the soft earth. They talked of God, the creator of all seeds; they wanted to find him, to see him. They had nothing to do but rest and talk all winter long. They grew lonely and longed for the spring when they would grow up out of the ground and begin to reach up to heaven and find God. They finally went to sleep.

Soon it was spring. The warm sun waked them up. Each seed burst from its shell and began to grow up and down. As the roots pushed down the green bud pushed up. When they slipped into the sunlight and blinked at the sky, it seemed a long, long way to heaven. But as they grew taller and reached out toward the heavenly blue, their little hands clutched the air in vain, for it would not sustain them. Their long green bodies were so thin and weak they fell back to the earth again and again. The two sweet peas were very sad, for they realized they would never see God, never find him at all.

One day a little boy came along, whistling a bright tune. He saw the sweet peas lying on the ground exhausted and discouraged and he exclaimed, "What beautiful flowers," for by this time their colors were pink and white, very pretty together. The boy started to pick them. The sweet peas grew alert. Hope revived. "Now is the time," they said, "to try again to reach up to heaven. We'll get the boy to help us." So they asked the friendly little boy to help them touch the sky. This was quite a problem for such a young lad. He thought and thought and thought. At last he decided what he could do to help. He reached into his pocket and pulled out some stout string and a shiny new knife. He picked up two dead branches and trimmed them to sharp points which he stuck deep into the ground. He stretched the string between and around the sticks. Then he wrapped the sweet peas' tiny hands around the string. The little boy then hopped away to his whistled tune.

The sweet peas clutched the string and began to grow up and up, climbing higher and higher. "We'll soon reach heaven," they said, and traveled the string around and around the sticks. They were very happy. "Surely we'll see God at last." But suddenly they were startled by a voice. It was God's voice. They had found him and his heaven at last. But God said:

"It is my will for you to stay where you are, to continue to grow, so that you may beautify your spot of earth and make it seem almost like heaven. Without the flowers man might forget to love beauty. Heaven is wherever I am, and I am here with you so long as you use your life to grow and flower in the way I intended from the beginning of your life."

So the two little sweet peas obeyed God and there they are to this day, making their bit of earth more like heaven.

We are like those sweet peas. We, too, want to find God. But we must learn, as they did, that heaven and God are both near at hand when we use our life to make things more beautiful where we are. That is part of God's will for us.

Big Ears

Grown folks sometimes say, "Little pitchers have big ears." They mean that children hear more than grow-ups think they do. Children can hear a lot when they keep their ears open. The ears are like doors to your brain house. They let in all sorts of wonderful things when they are open.

We all have ears, haven't we? Let's see. Feel of them; pull them. Ouch! Now we know we have two ears each. What do we do with them? We listen and we hear. Can you hear me? That means your ear doors are open and the word sounds are coming in. What would happen if you couldn't hear? Put your hands over your ears — close the ear doors. Now what do you hear? (Speak very softly.) Nothing! Well, maybe a little, but not as much as when your ears are open. It's just as though you had a real door in each ear labeled, "Open for business, come in."

We hear all right just as we are. But we can hear even better when we cup our ears, like a pitcher handle, and pay close attention. Try it. (Speak loudly.) Do you think I look like a pitcher?

I've told you about ears and pitchers because this year our ears will be very important. Since we have ears we can listen and hear. Since we have two ears and only one mouth, we should listen twice as much as we speak. If we listen all through the year we shall fill up the pitcher — our minds and hearts — with some of the things God wants us to know and do. Jesus said, "He that hath ears to hear, let him hear." (Mark 4:9)

If we listen carefully, we shall have something wonderfully good to pour from the spout of our pitcher and God will give us many new ways to express our love for him by obeying him when we hear his voice.

Little pitchers, use your ears.

*   *   *

Two stories for adults show how the medium of storytelling is just as effective for them as it is for children.

Christmas Carol in Story Form

This is the story song of Jason and the candles and the two stars in the sky, and of what happened on the night Jesus was born. This carol in story form is spoken in remembrance of Him whose birth brought a million new stars into the sky of man's life, and whose life blessed with infinite compassion all mankind forever after.

Jason was a shepherd boy who loved the great open spaces of nature, the rugged chill of wintry, wind-swept nights and, best of all, the beckoning of the stars. He loved his sheep also and tended them well, protecting them and caring for them. Jason was a Hebrew lad who had learned of God and worshiped him. He found God very close and wonderful as night after night he dreamed and in his dreaming explored the vast reaches of heaven. But he loved the stars best; they were so friendly. Some were joyful and twinkling; others were solemn and still. He loved them all but he was partial to the twinkling ones, and often called them his candles of the sky. Occasionally some of the stars would fall as golden streams before his eyes — these he liked to think of as dripping, fiery tallow which spilled from his brightly burning candles of the sky. Other stars dimmed and brightened as the wind fanned them by, at least so he liked to imagine. So far away, yet so close to his heart, were these tiny jewels of the sky.

One night, calm and clear and cold, he was gazing as usual toward his favorite stars, trying with all the power of his mind to carry himself to them, when suddenly two of the brightest ones moved — yes, moved — closer and closer together, until finally they merged as one brilliant flame. Jason marvelled at the strange and beautiful sight, for he had never seen the like of it before. He wondered why it had happened. It worried him for days, because the next night the star was gone, and though he watched and watched, never once did that particular big, bright star appear.

One year later, on the very night the star had first appeared, Jason had a glorious dream. He dreamed he was in a huge temple, splendid with all the beauties and riches man could devise, execute, and gather. Great waves of angelic music, singing, and incense overwhelmed him. He found himself all alone, kneeling before the immense and wondrously wrought altar of the temple. But instead of the usual sacrifice, he saw two candles burning and between them stood a cross. As he watched in awesome wonder, the music swelled to a tremendous climax and the whole scene swam before his eyes. Then the two candles floated together and merged their flames as one dazzling brightness, that seemed to center in the cross. And, lo, Jason knew it was the two stars merged again as one.

Jason never forgot the stars and the dream. And each year, on the anniversary of his dream and the star's appearing, he placed two hand-fashioned candles upon a rude altar and between them a rough cross, and lighted them in memory of an event he knew must have come from God, it was so wonderful. And Jason worshiped God more readily than ever before at his altar. And yet Jason never really knew the true meaning of it all nor did he understand the strange new feelings in his heart until many years later when a man named Paul told him the story of the Messiah, who had been born that night in the very country where he had been. Paul told him of the child who was both God and man. It was only then that Jason understood. For he had received the answer to all his questions concerning the two flames — his candles and his stars becoming as one — and the deep longings of his heart were satisfied forever after.

Twin candles burn tonight on the altar for the Lord Jesus. His birth gave flame to the first candle, the little human star; his birth also gave flame to the second candle, the star divine. It seems in remembrance as if God and man were emerging, not God alone nor man alone, but as the fusion of God's all-pervading love and man's receptive nature. As we think of it all tonight, it seems as if God alone was too far away and man alone was too insufficient, as if the gift and the giver must become one. So tonight the candles burn for God and man united in one — Christ. And the candles *will* merge as we gaze at them, will center in the cross, burning brightly and steadily as one, until the end of time.

We burn candles this night because of Jesus and we are

able to say because of him that the candle is the body, the flame is its life, and the vapor from the burning is its spirit. The flame melts the tallow, dissolving it into vapor, which floats into every crevice of man's life.

We have told a carol in story form. May it become a song that will sing in our hearts and continue its blessing as it did for Jason through all the years.

The Legend of the Bird

Once upon a time there was a wise man, a very wise man, who could answer any question asked of him. A woman who heard of his great gift decided that surely there must be some question he could not answer. She thought and she thought, and finally found a question she knew the wise man could not answer. She said to herself, " I will take a live bird in my hand and go to the wise man and ask him, ' Is the bird I hold in my hand alive or dead? ' and if he says alive, I will squeeze the life out of it; but if he says dead, I will release it. In either case I shall prove him wrong."

So the woman made the journey to the wise man, knowing that at last she had a question he could not answer. She came into his presence with the bird held behind her and she said, " O Wise Man, I have a question to ask of thee "; and the wise man said, "Ask and I shall answer." So she asked her question, " Is the bird I hold in my hand alive or dead? " The wise man pondered for a moment and then he replied, " Only you can tell." So the wise man kept his reputation intact by giving the correct answer to the woman's question.

CHAPTER IV

THE ESSAY

A word fitly spoken is like apples of gold in pictures of silver.
PROVERBS 25:11

THE ESSAY form is used by the clergyman in many ways: quite commonly as a section of the weekly bulletin; as an annual *apologia* for fund-raising in letters and printed matter; in teaching through specially prepared forms and bulletins and leaflets (this is particularly true with reference to the area of Christian education); infrequently as an article or column for the newspaper, one of the denominational papers or magazines. I append several samples of this form of ministry through the reasoned word, attempting to point up the value of comparatively succinct utterance for unraveling or developing a single thought. An essay is really a form of meditation, for it seeks to reveal more of the truth about a word, an idea, or an incident. Some of the following are imaginative and poetic, some are in the style of analogue, the rest are in straight prose.

Practically all of the short essays were written as the parson's corner of the weekly parish paper. Several of them were published later in magazines. All of them helped the writer to keep his hand moving to the rhythm of his thoughts and to keep fresh the inspirations which came.

The Place of Women in the Life of the Parish

When theorizing about parish responsibility, we think in terms of an equal sharing in that responsibility by every communicant of the parish. Actually, however, this is nothing but an ideal; but we are hoping that some plan will eventually remedy this grave defect in the structure and fabric of our parish life. When we come to the present-day facts and face them, we find the usual state of affairs to be somewhat as follows: the rector is the leader in all activities and is rightfully the director of all policies. Normally the vestry would come next, but we find the average vestry limiting its interest more or less to the financial problems of the parish. If we come right down to the backbone of both the work and worship of the parish, we find it inevitably to be the church women in their several organizations. It is true, the young people play an important part, as do the other organizations and individuals, but the church women in reality hold the parish together.

As to the women being an " auxiliary " to the life of the church, we could more truthfully say they are " primarily " the life of the church. In the first place, the average woman is more thoroughly consecrated to the work of the church than either the men or the young people. Perhaps this comes out of her age-old role of mother-wife, the strength and binding-power of every family. She is the chief minister of all goodness and as such has taken on no mean responsibility for the growth of the kingdom of God. Second (and this comes out of the first), the women of the parish are eager to take hold of any problem and see that it is solved, because they realize how important it is to their family and the families of the world. Third, they are the guardians of every good work and every responsibility placed upon the parish by the diocese, the province, the national church, the community, the state, the nation, or by any other authority. We might say they are the dependability undergirding every forward-moving effort. Fourth, without them the rector's hands would be tied but with them he has at his fingertips enough energy, wisdom, fidelity, and sacrifice to touch the rims of the earth with God's glory.

Perhaps we should be more practical and enumerate a thousand and one chores which the women do with joy; but every task, no matter what it is, when it is lifted up and dedicated to God's service, is a worthy expression of one's desire to follow Christ. So we add, in summary, that the place of the women in the life of the parish is primarily to carry out the work assigned or uncovered for meeting every known need in the spirit of Christ. The name by which we call them doesn't matter but the spirit of their labor does. Through the years the names may change but the spirit never.

A Latticed Fence

All during Lent we have been in a garden surrounded by a latticed fence. At brief intervals we have caught snatches of squared sunlight squeezing itself into blocks of cheerfulness to slip through the white lattice. We have hungered for more light. We were not content with stealing squares. But if it had not been for the glimpses of truant gold, our eyes would have been blinded by the brilliance of Easter dawn, with its sheet of dazzling flame. We have been prepared for light by seeping sparkles in the darkness.

Many of us have always lived in a garden surrounded by a latticed fence. All we know about life on the outside is that it is made up of jigsaw puzzles, with half of the pieces missing. We are confused by dancing squares behind the never-moving strips of white. Perhaps our fence has a gate. It will be hard to open if it has never been used. But it can be opened, and unless it is, we shall continue to remain inside a garden of unfulfilled desires and useless longings.

Lent begins inside the latticed fence, but it leads through the gate out into the world of people and things and God. Easter is the passport to the continued brightness of tomorrow and tomorrow. Leave your sackcloth and ashes in

the garden and come into the brightness of a new life clothed
in brilliant white garments of praise and thanksgiving.

The Crooked Path of Destiny

It was nothing less than a miracle of God that brought me
at last to the decision to be a minister. My friends and my
family had given up all hope concerning my future. They
felt I would probably turn out to be a wishy-washy ne'er-
do-well. There were pretty good grounds for that, too.
Everything I tried my hand at lost its allure, right early.
I had dreamed of being an electrical engineer, but at Texas
Agricultural and Mechanical College the dullness of the
theory, in contrast with the thrill of the practical end of it
which I had experienced as a motion-picture projectionist
and lowly member of a power-plant repair crew, bored me
and cooled my enthusiasm. I " quitchuated."

Then followed incident after incident in scatter-brained
fashion. A year was spent as office boy for an insurance
company (all my menfolk were insurance men) but I grew
restless under the deadly routine of it. Because my father
wanted me to be a lawyer, I went to night law school for a
year. It, too, failed to capture my imagination. At the same
time *The Little Theater* movement fired my enthusiasm to
white-hot pitch, and I put heart and soul into this for a time
under Oliver Hinsdell in the little green house on Olive
Street, Dallas, Texas, with brief excursions into stock and
summer artist colonies. It too began to pale.

Then music became a passion and for two years I was its
willing slave: piano, voice, organ, theory, composition and
the like, from early morning until late at night. During this
period I began singing in the choir of an Episcopal church
and a new world was opened to me. From that moment on
I knew I belonged in the church. The beauty and dignity

were a wonderful contrast to the rather barren church in which I had grown up. I became interested in the music at St. Matthew's Children's Home and St. Andrew's Mission, through the Brotherhood of St. Andrew (both in Dallas, Texas), and gave much of my time to both places.

During my two years of this work among the under-privileged in the cotton-mill district of South Dallas, the moving purpose of my life was made clearly known to me. I had been a lay minister during much of the time, and even this brought me face to face with the power and need of the Christian religion in these often miserable and tangled lives. I knew I must go on and become a minister, even though I struggled hard and long over the final decision to let my music go.

After clearing up most of my needed credits for a liberal arts degree at the University of Colorado, I snapped up the chance to become organist and chapelmaster at the newly re-opened Western Theological Seminary in Evanston, Illinois.

Seminary was a great disappointment. I had a vision glorious of fire from heaven constantly glowing upon the heads of both professors and students, and believed that every time I knelt in prayer I would hear the angels sing. I was disillusioned, even though our little private strip of street was called "Haven" — which was, incidentally, the inspiration later for my daily radio program. The chief fault was with myself, I learned later on, and not with the seminary. I had been so naïve and ignorant that the process of modern theological education had startled and confused me for the first year or so.

My early ministry suffered because I had not been ade-quately prepared for my life in the seminary, and I had not taken advantage of all the opportunities at hand during my stay there. My language preparation was especially faulty and led to much misery. My eyes were barely opened to the opportunities and to my deep spiritual needs, and I missed most of the rich spiritual treasures available. Two men influenced me tremendously, however. One was Dr. Fuller of Garrett Biblical Institute, who gave me a vision and an understanding of the Bible and made it a practical tool for me. This is the nearest I came to seeing fire on a professor's head and hearing angels singing within. The other one was Dr. Frederick C. Grant, my dean, professor, and good friend, who gave me a vision of the practical end of the ministry; and I have never forgotten his many wise admonitions for a well-rounded life, even though I have not remembered all of the synoptic problems he discussed so brilliantly.

By now you will be wondering, what's the point and why the title? The point is that God drives us hard until we heed his call. We must be willing to follow where he leads if we would find our place in his plan. " Destiny " of course, is the wrong word, but by it I mean God's plan for us at last fulfilled. No square pegs in round holes, if we continue to seek, ask, and knock until the way is opened. When we see our niche we shall know. When the vision comes, soon or late, and we follow it, we shall become God's instruments and we shall find genuine joy in helping to maintain the fabric of the world, for in the handiwork of our craft, our calling, is our prayer and our rightful place.

We Begin a New Christian Year Together

Each week during the year we shall have a brief chat together about the more important matters of God's kingdom here in this parish.

Let us begin by emphasizing the putting of first things first and the constant relating of the Christian way of life to every phase of our daily living.

There are many things to do, and with God's help we shall do them as we work together as one unit.

Our supreme task is first of all to grow spiritually ourselves and then to aid others, by sharing what we have learned and experienced with them.

We shall endeavor to keep a high challenge before us and so to present reality that others will come to be inspired by the same challenge.

There must be no stumbling-blocks put in the way of our progress or our responsibility to the community or to the church at large. We must surrender all petty and narrow viewpoints for the greater good.

There will be no misunderstandings if from the beginning we are honest with each other. If anything happens which is not understood, come to me for the reason back of it. Do not repeat and enlarge upon differences until true and correct knowledge is known.

In my sermon this morning I have tried to point out the way my ministry is going to travel while here with you, but I can do nothing alone. We shall all be bound by the great obligation of the churchman's bounden duty.

" My bounden duty is to *follow* Christ, to *worship* God every Sunday in his church, and to *work* and *pray* and *give* for the spread of his kingdom."

In Time of Illness

There has been so much sickness in the parish, it has been well-nigh impossible to keep up with all who have been ill. But I have been thinking of each sick person and have been keeping in touch through daily prayer. Here are a few suggestions for changing the time presumably " lost " into an everlasting benefit.

First: Relax and let Nature have all its powers for fighting the alien virus coursing through our bodies and whipping up the fire. In other words, allow God's healing to do its work of re-creation. This will require patience. Patience, by the by, is nothing more than dependence upon God, and is gained by practice.

Second: Concentrate, when feelings permit, on neglected areas of thinking and acting. Here is a chance for much needed reflection and plans for restoration. Watch this or it may become morbidity. Self is pretty much a sore thumb when we are sick. However, no reflection ever becomes morbid when we keep within the range of our mental vision the others who are always a part of the complete picture. Illness has sometimes descended as a blessing when man discovers his selfishness in such a convincing way that it produces results.

Third: Make use of your time as sickness goes. Catch up on that overdue conversation between husband and wife, or parent and child, or between self and pastor. When the mind is no longer merry-go-rounding, use it for planning steps to take when strength is restored. Precious moments of companionship may slip away, if we do not catch them as they flow past.

Fourth: Leave your business in the hands of someone else. Accept a shot of humility as you realize that it will probably get along beautifully without you — a hard but necessary lesson for one's ego to learn.

The Sermon and You

The sermon this morning is not intended to be profound but merely to be a peep into human nature and a dip into human experience. Impatience is a common human ailment which, like a cold, rarely ever causes death, except when it runs into complications; but, like the cold, it is widely prevalent and unpleasant, and causes a great deal of unnecessary suffering and loss of effectiveness. As always, when listening to a sermon, there should be some guidelines for the mind to follow. For this particular sermon the following suggestions may prove profitable:

1. Keep the subject — patience — always in focus in relation to yourself. Never let another person creep into central focus and push you into the background or out of the picture.

2. Jot down in the blank spaces on this bulletin certain thoughts, which offer hope of conquering impatience for you, and other thoughts which give you insight into the causes of your impatience.

3. Remember especially the gist of the personal illustrations, for they come from our common experience.

The final test of the "goodness" of a sermon is its effectiveness in meeting an individual's need. "Patience and How to Have It" must produce patience in those who hear and heed, or else it is not "good" for them.

Symptoms Are Not Sins

There have been some requests for last Sunday's sermon on "Symptoms Are Not Sins." Since the sermon was preached from an outline and not from a verbatim copy, I should like to summarize it for all who found it of value:

"Symptoms are the outward and visible evidences of the inward and often invisible sin. Social symptoms such as war and unemployment; individual symptoms such as resentments, anxieties, muddled thinking, adultery, gambling, drink, lethargy — these are the results of the real causes deep down: the fear, unrest, distrust, disruption, rationalization, desire to escape, which come when God has spoken to us and we have disobeyed, when the choice has been for self as god. All symptoms are futile attempts to escape facing this reality of self. The cure is obedience at every point of crisis, and the stripping away of every layer which covers up the seed of life at the center. From the Master Physician we learn both the cause and the cure. If Christ is not living for you, and if your faith is not placed in his living, loving presence, you are still under the control of your sins and are spending your doctoring time on your symptoms where it will do no good.

" Self is the evil, the sin. Remove its prominence and the real self will be revealed. Jesus insures freedom through his resurrection in us, if we adopt the scientific life principle of self-surrender — that is, give up preconceptions and be led along by the facts. All of which means a willingness to *do* as God directs from now on, until ' there is no longer room for sin.'

"Are you still under the control of your sins? Well? "

What Lies Ahead?

The New Year confronts us with the joyous task of meeting the needs of everyone in the parish. This parish is a constant source of stimulation and challenge. For there are enough of the older ones, steeped in the rich tradition of the past, to give the parish balance, stability, and continuity; there are also enough of the newer, younger ones, eager for change and newness, to give it life and color. We shall meet the needs of the former and those of the latter by a fine Christian balance, simple and dignified enough to connect with the past but different and moving enough to point a direction toward future accomplishment.

Our " first thing " always is to create daily the fresh out-pouring of love one for the other, in mutual consideration and understanding each of the other's beliefs and modes of worship. There can be no harmonious and united whole without the firm adherence of all the parts. This parish has had a glorious and deep-rooted past which will become the inspiration and guide for its destined future. May God always be near unto us and direct us according to his will.

Being On Time

Each service of the Prayer Book is a unit planned in ascending and developing order. Each part depends upon every other part. If the first part is missed, the second part will be the less valuable because unprepared for; or if the sixth part is missed, the fifth part will lose much of its meaning and all of its climax. If we grow careless about our time schedule on Sunday morning, we frequently miss step one in the morning service of worship.

The unmatched values of being on time for each service — of course with the occasional exceptions of accident, earthquake, fire, or flood — will give us all we ought to expect and ask from a service of worship.

No matter what household routine has interfered (barring occasional slips) it could be cured by starting five or ten minutes earlier. This is one simple discipline, the practice of which will add tremendously to the value of every Sunday: *Better late than never, but never late is better.*

Salvation

"Salvation" (or "redemption") is more than a pious word for a crowd on a street corner to hear and ponder. It is the "pituitary gland" of the spirit. If the army of Christ ever marches to the tune of "Onward, Christian

Soldiers," the banner out in front will be colored by " salvation " and marked with " redemption." Grand is the sound of " world redemption " (or " world salvation "); but when will it be, how will it come, who will see to it? The symbol of salvation-redemption is the cross upon which one life was stretched to the limit of self-giving. This means that when we place this symbol before us, the stark outlines of its truth convict us and show us the reach of self-giving which must be striven after, before at-one-ment with God becomes fact. Salvation, then, means a personal deliverance from the bondage of sin (self-clinging) and from the self-inflicted penalties for violating God's laws. It is freedom from this self-clinging, and it delimits our life in all directions. It is that long haul upward out of our human directed morass, which begins with self-surrender and ends with God-self-possession.

Jesus seems to say that salvation is the process of changing and liberating a mind, so that it can rise to and live on the glory level. Redemption is the paying of a price sufficient to buy back and repossess something sold below its true value. It is, in a simple way, the realization that the price tag the world has placed upon life has been too low, and that a Man is waiting upon a cross to buy it back and put a higher price tag on it. Jesus seems to say keep the tag of right worth on everything.

How far away is the world's redemption? Just as far as our minds are from the mind of Christ. Just as far as our hearts are from the hearts of others. " Salvation," " redemption," either word will do to describe the miracle of deliverance which began its continuous activity at that moment when Jesus gave away his right to himself in order that man might be one with God. The " when " and the " how " both find answers the moment our minds coincide with Christ's mind; and God and the world will see it.

Security

" Security " is a relative word and is used in a multitude of ways. Everyone wants it. Not everyone has it. To some it means a permanent job and a steady income. To another it means a tidy sum in the bank. To another it is a plot of ground with a house on it. To another it is a card. To another it is insurance. To another it is health. To another it is government bonds. To another it is the love of someone. But not in money, not in houses, not even in nations, can we find the real security man's heart demands.

Jesus meant it when he said: " Do not store up your riches on earth, where moths and rust destroy them, and where thieves break in and steal them, but store up your riches in heaven, where moths and rust cannot destroy them, and where thieves cannot break in and steal them. For wherever your treasure is, your heart will be also." (Matthew 6:19-21)[1]

Real security depends upon our placing our faith in imperishable things, such as truth, justice, love, and integrity. These things are among man's highest treasures and come from God. Man must place his active trust in these as the determining factors in the world's becoming an abiding place for the qualities of the Kingdom life.

Nothing material is stable. There is one anchor only — God. There is one sure sign — Christ. There is one perfect hope — man's history. That which is spiritually high and strong has endured. All else has passed away. The Chinese say, " This, too, will pass." In the long period of their civilization, everything which ministered to man's lower, baser nature has turned to dust. Only that which has called out man's highest and best has endured.

[1] From *The Bible, An American Translation,* by Smith and Goodspeed. Used by permission of the University of Chicago Press.

Security consists not in the abundance of the things we possess but in the magnitude of our love and unselfishness and faith. Only he who lives on the strength of the latter will be " without care " (this is what security really means) and find his heart in the place of all real treasure, the presence of God.

Roots

" These good people are so rootless."

I read these words in an article concerned primarily with the vanishing virtues of Christianity in professed Christians, which the author calls " the apostasy of American Protestants." Not that these " apostates " are evil livers necessarily, but that they have not taken their religion seriously enough and that they let the slightest excuse prevent them from practicing it. They too frequently, for example, make going to church elective. This is true time and again when choices made and excuses (" reasons ") given win out. They don't go to church because " they don't like the minister, or they are not greeted with sufficient sociability, or they just don't feel like going to church today." Sleep — it is the only morning for it, you know; the Sunday paper — it must be read before noon, of course; fooling with the car; beaches and other spots come out the winner in many people's lives.

Lack of regular church attendance is only a symptom of a deeper disease, an unrelated rootlessness, where individualism has gotten beyond its reasonable limits. The corporate fellowship of the church frees us from the spiritually weakening disease of subjectivism and keeps ever before us objective reality as the balance wheel of salvation. We are flirting with Christianity's doom when we allow the whims of " my will " to push aside our faithful duty to love God with all our hearts, souls, and minds and our fellow man as ourselves.

Jesus planted deep the roots of the requirements of discipleship and made as the first principle of the religious life: " If any man would be my disciple let him deny himself and take up his cross and follow me."

" . . . these good people are so rootless," because they have never yet allowed God's spirit to dwell in them.

Warm Welcome

Someone seems to be always coming to the fore and saying, " But I just can't greet a perfect stranger in church." My answer follows herewith in an attempt to make clear how anyone can greet a stranger in church without undue agony or ill effects.

Our greeting depends first on our inner attitude. We must really *want* to greet the stranger and welcome him into the worshiping fellowship. The warmth of our greeting depends upon the warmth of our affection. But the inner desire alone is not enough. It must be reflected in our face, our smile, and in our handclasp.

" But I just couldn't bear it if I greeted someone who turned out to be a regular member of the parish." Nonsense! Thank God that at last you have met, and ask his forgiveness for being a stranger so long within the same fellowship.

" What shall I say? " There can be no set rule. Your name would be given first. The stranger would respond. Be sure you give your name clearly and understand his. Welcome him and perhaps ask him if he is a stranger in the city. If he is a newcomer or unattached, ask him to fill in a visitor's card. Introduce him to persons near at hand, preferably ones his own age. Part in a friendly fashion and urge his return. Make a mental note to keep a lookout for him. Perhaps plan to pay him a visit, or invite him to a midweek meeting, if there is one for him. Lose no time in making the stranger feel less strange and that your parish church is the place for him. We can measure the rapidity of our growth by the temperature of our greeting. One family recently added to the parish came in primarily because of the warm greeting of a member. Every person who comes to a service is a potential member and recruit for this company of Christ's army.

Try today. Practice makes more expert. God needs us to win others.

The World Scene
from the Vantage Point of Eternity

The season of Advent is all tied up with "judgment," "death," and "second coming." That is why it is a penitential season. What better time could we find for thinking honestly concerning the events of our day than this season? We must ponder the great Advent phrases of "when He shall come to judge," "ever hold fast the blessed hope," "prepare and make ready thy way," "speedily help and deliver us," to find the answers. We find this season more concerned with the unpleasant duties of sinful man's needs than with holly and snow.

But we plunge from the almost gloomy atmosphere of Advent into the bright night of God's Son's birth. What makes those days of wrath and days of mourning suddenly change to angels singing and stars shining? If we discover this, we shall find the secret passageway from sorrow to joy, from darkness to light.

Advent's message is of Christ's coming, and the mere anticipation of his brightness makes the present without him unutterably dark, and this is his judgment. As we look for him, we find barriers in ourselves, and the whole of Advent must be given to their removal; for as we see him in prospect, he judges us, but his judgment is the blessed hope of restoration in his birth.

Therefore, as we prepare and make ready Christ's way, he will speedily help and deliver us from our present life, which is death in contrast.

More simply put, Advent is the great panorama of man's doom, which stands as a warning and boldly proclaims, " this is your life without Christ." The very sight of it presses us on faster and faster toward Christmas Day, when we hungrily and lovingly receive his spirit within and turn our backs on the promise because it has become the fulfillment.

More Than Bread

How often have men yearned for a repetition of the miracle of " the loaves." Bread has become for many today the *luxury* rather than the *necessity* of life. Those who have known hunger, sharp pains and squirmings in the stomach, can picture with vivid reality the people following Jesus for days, sustained only by the glory of his words, suddenly awakening to their bodily needs. Jesus understood their plight and did something about it. " I pity these people, for they have been staying with me three days now, and they have nothing left to eat. And if I send them home hungry they will give out on the way, for some of them come from a distance." (Mark 8:2, 3)[1] Jesus was first of all concerned for the welfare of his people. He not only possessed understanding but foresight as well. He saw them " all the way home."

If we were concerned enough today, the desperate conditions of peoples, whether of hunger, of homelessness, or of bondage, would be remedied much faster than they are.

[1] From *The Bible, An American Translation,* by Smith and Goodspeed. Used by permission of the University of Chicago Press.

Where the right attitude of loving concern exists, miracles can always be wrought. But man must become a flame rather than a heat-wilted candle. Jesus taught by miracles because he realized that they were always possible when the hearts and minds of men were deeply enough concerned.

Magic words and wands are not the source of power for miracles. Love is! Jesus had more than enough. We need much more. Trinity season is well under way. May God the Father, God the Son, and God the Holy Spirit find expression through us in miracles " of loaves."

Highways

Publicity means news about something, and the right kind of publicity always means good news. Publicity is, therefore, peculiarly a thing to be placed at the service of the church, for the gospel is really, actually, good news.

Of course, it is sometimes difficult to realize this when we listen to a sermon or shadow a Christian. But Jesus deliberately trusted the success of his ministry to publicity. Everything that bears witness to Jesus Christ has publicity content and effect.

The physical existence of the church, the whole body of believers, is a continuing witness. Every active Christian is an advertisement. Every inactive Christian is an advertisement too, an advertisement *against* the cause of Christ. The spire and the bell, the hospital and the school desk, the worship and the work, and all the visible possessions of the church help to convey the Christian message.

Perhaps we had better give a more formal definition of church publicity: " Church publicity is the process of making information public, to the end that men's opinions and conduct may be influenced toward the purposes for which the church exists."

Therefore church publicity is a means of *education*, and of *evangelization*. Whether a particular publicity effort takes the form of a periodical, a handbill, a bulletin, a letter, an advertisement, or a sermon, it is not fulfilling its mission unless it carries its informative message (education), and in addition, a portion of the " good news " (evangelization) that the church has to tell the world.

A simple formula for church advertising: *Belief* plus *knowledge* equals *action*.

How utterly uninteresting and impossible is a journey upon a highway enclosed by high walls. There is no color, only darkness; there is no trace of joy and freedom. Certainly it could never be called the road to the kingdom of God, no matter how straight and narrow it might be. Instead of this, we should find all along the way, as " billboards of the Holy Spirit," glimpses of the church's mission, what the church is doing, what the church needs to do, crystal-clear statements of the church's belief. This takes us back to the formula. Belief is blind without knowledge. Knowledge is impotent without belief. Combined, they witness to the life of any God-man.

CHAPTER V

POETRY AND PRAYER

Singing with grace in your hearts to the Lord.
COLOSSIANS 3:16

TREAD LIGHTLY here, though a great deal of our so-called poetry is prose arranged in blank verse form or else a rhyming doggerel which is fairly easy for us all. I know clergymen who think almost in the form of limerick and can give you one on any subject while you wait. There are others who constantly write rhymes and nonsensical verse. Probably none of us can be classified as a poet, but we can all use the discipline and beauty and depth perception of the form to express a little better the almost inexpressible perceptions which come to us at certain times and seasons.

A Wisp of Straw — Christmas

A wisp of straw laid in a manger
All because a tiny Babe had to have a bed . . .
Had to have a bed for sleep
Under a happy, starry sky . . .
The story of a beginning . . .
Never yet a sequel of an ending!
A tinge of coolness . . .
Far away, a star . . .
Close by, quietness . . .
Simple the setting
For the birth of the Savior
Of a world!

We celebrate this Mass of Christ
In remembrance of a beginning!

The Poet of Assisi — Saint Francis

I

A merchant's son must play with cloth: cloth of bright and shining colors; cloth of gold and cloth of silver; cloth of richest velvet smoothness; cloth of warmest fleecy wool.

A cloth-merchant's son, born about 1181, was christened Giovanni Bernadone. His father's business furnished his toys — rags and tags of fascinating cloth, odds and ends of future adornment-glory.

Priests at baptism speak our names and bind us to their often irksome fetters. But we sometimes change them and smile. Giovanni became Francesco, became Francis, became St. Francis.

Have all saints first been sinners? St. Francis was once a waster. His wares were dancing and gaiety and not cloth. The cloth-merchant's son sold not cloth but disgrace. Francis received his eager, joyous heart from his mother.

The rhythmic pattern of his youth was mischief, revelry, revelry mischief; but the sunny days sped by and were soon forgotten. For war came. Francesco became a follower of the flashing arms. They dimmed in the prison at Perugia where the prisoner's babyhood memories fluttered gaily — still colored cloth, free for the taking. Francis had not changed.

But facing death transmutes. A serious illness finally brought him out of the wilderness of his own disharmony. Francesco grew to believe in Christ, to remember his sins, to think of others, to become recklessly compassionate.

His own confession: " When I was yet in my sins it did seem to me too bitter to look upon lepers, but the Lord himself did lead me among them, and I had compassion upon them. When I left them, that which had seemed to me bitter had become sweet and easy."

II

No more cloth in prospect to sell, no more contact with his earthly father, for home ties were broken. Vows were taken. " Give all that thou hast . . ." became a literal command to follow. Francis had his first vision of things to come on the road to Rome. God spake to him: " Restore the fallen house of God."

St. Domain was the first church restored. Two years were spent in Assisi, aiding the unfortunate and restoring churches. His favorite was the Portiuncula, in the plain outside the town.

His second vision came at the altar of this little church of the loving hands. It was his trumpet call to action: " Preach repentance and the kingdom of God." Without money, in the plainest garments, eating what might be set before him, he imitated Christ and obeyed Christ's commands implicitly. In absolute poverty, in Christlike love, he won many who followed him. Their rule became fixed from one of Christ's commands — the Humbler Brethren.

St. Francis was the first Vachel Lindsay. But Francis exchanged the godly rhymes of *his* soul for the ears and hearts of men. His minstrelsy turned faces upward. He made Jesus live again for the common people. He lived as in a perfect brotherhood. He gave us *The Canticle of the Sun*, showing his love of all God's creation and God's nature. To him all creatures had souls and loved. In this divine simplicity of his nature, we find his greatness.

Brother Sun and Sister Moon; Brother Wind and Sister Water; Brother Fire and Sister Earth; Sister Death. The birds – Little Brothers and Sisters of the Air, flying bits of colored string – ravelings from the past. He preached to them. They belonged to God. They were God.

Supreme in poetic utterance and poetic living, the little boy who had played with cloth was the cloth-merchant's son no longer. God had claimed him for his own.

III

He married quite literally Lady Poverty; and he was alone, cast off from the earth-rich realm of the silken cloth. His Friars Minor soon flooded the world. But his footsteps faltered. He found that adoration and meditation could not be carried in a sack, and these became his meat and drink. He retired more and more from the world.

Mount Alvernia became his sanctuary. His only protest to organization and church authority was a phrase to his brethren: " From henceforth I am dead to you."

In the singing green trees and the singing blue fountains, in the quiet pure heights of virgin stone, St. Francis climbed the ladder to Heaven.
One posture – on his knees.
One word – " My God."
Flesh no longer existed for him consciously. He had found the beauty and the majesty of complete forgetfulness of self. He had found a new rhythmic pattern for his life.

Prayer and singing; singing and prayer. Francis longed to be constantly present with Christ. He was.

IV

" I in Christ and Christ in me." Few have understood this phrase of Paul's. The world stands between Christ and us.

But the true love of Christ perfectly transformed St. Francis. He was completely absorbed into God and into the true image of Christ crucified. The world was forgotten.

So intense, so complete, was Giovanni's love and desire to share all with Christ, that he prayed without ceasing to know the pain of his beloved Master's most bitter passion. The Miracle of the Stigmata in his hands and in his feet bore mute witness to the fact: he shared the sacred wounds of Christ. One of the nearest of mortal men to Jesus.

He died, yet did not die. He had already become a familiar figure in the heavenly places long before his poor body received the tears of those who knew him not.

Raised as a monument to his conversion, the Portiuncula became the haven of his last spiritual pilgrimage. He carried the marks of the Lord Jesus in his hands, in his feet, and in his side.

The pretty bits of cloth had faded now, but in their place remnants of God's glory in St. Francis still shine.

Epilogue

If " a poet is one who can truly see beauty within the blackest mire, who takes the common things of life and clothes their nakedness with fire," then St. Francis is a poet.

If a poet is one who can reveal the inmost secrets of nature, make vivid the common soil, and convince man of its sanctity, then St. Francis is a poet.

If a poet is one who can crystallize experience into an immortal reality, giving it the tinge of remembered understanding, then St. Francis is a poet.

If a poet is one who can enshrine the best of life in a thought-action, can catch in stone the flash of an idea, can implant abiding principles, can arouse to fervor and ecstasy, then St. Francis is a poet whose voice was the expression of his life, and whose gospel of beauty was preached in his sermons of prayer.

No one man has ascended to such heights, and has ever been able to draw others up to his far-reaching vista, except St. Francis.

A poet exists to lift men up, to quiet men's hearts, to beckon men on, to inspire and make livable the day-by-day existence of man.

St. Francis was a poet. His greatest poem we might name, *Come, Jesu!* His next greatest, *Ah, Nature!*

Posterity, man and man, has named his winsome loveliness as " next to Jesus."

> Singing the song of a humble man,
>   Praying the prayer of a sinner;
> Changing the wealth of the world for sores,
>   Preaching the love of God.
>
> Singing the song of a happy man,
>   Praying the prayer of repentance;
> Changing the wealth of the world for peace,
>   Preaching the love of God.
>
> Singing the song of a saintly man,
>   Praying the prayer of forgiveness;
> Changing the wealth of the world for souls,
>   Preaching the love of God.

The Spirit of Christmas

It was chilly that night in Bethlehem.

The crisp, clear air pulled cloaks tightly around shivering shoulders.

The shepherds marvelled at the starlit beauty of the night.

It seemed, almost, as if the world had been cleansed by an unforgettable radiance — and they felt it.

Some followed their restless urge toward a glowing, happy manger;

Others breathed the life-giving splendor of that night and knew not whence came the strange exhilaration in their souls.

Not much excitement over this Holy Babe then, but soon rumbles of Herod came from afar.

Both love and hate watched over His cradle — and they hovered, following, watching hungrily throughout His life.

Had love been the weaker, the failure of Christmas would have been absolute — but it was stronger!

Jesus entangled his godliness with the human heart — forever.

So Christmas, a quiet, lovely festival of hearts all tangled and intertwined — woven into a pattern — each individual self submerged in the burst of joyful sound . . .

"Good will . . ."

"Good will . . ."

Wild bells ringing, Lord Jesus.

"Good will . . ."

"Good will . . ."

To all mankind they 'claim.

And peace . . .

Earth's approach to heaven!

*   *   *

A greatly neglected field is hymn writing. Perhaps we should all work on this and create for our age the songs which will sing well to the tunes we have at hand. Like the poet Shelley we should write regularly, so that when a great flash of insight comes our pen will allow a flow of words, without thought as to technique.

One attempt at a long poem came from the realization that the ex-service men, with their unsolved problems, would not go to anyone for counsel, certainly not the parson, unless their war experience with chaplains had been particularly fine. The need, then, was for some word of counsel which could be slipped into the young man's mind almost without having him know. So *Hey Buddy* was written. I give a few excerpts from this poem-dialogue between two ex-service men, which has found widespread use in veterans' hospitals through the American Red Cross.

Hey Buddy

(This conversation takes place between two World War II veterans. The older one saw service in 1942 and part of 1943, and at the age of thirty-eight was honorably discharged; and by the time he meets the youngster, just returned from two years across, he has adjusted to civilian life and has found some of the answers to the problems of the ex-service man, which he attempts to pass along. A park bench in a coastal city furnishes the setting.)

My Padre was a good egg.
How about yours, Buddy?
A rotter, huh, a milksop? That's too bad.
You should have had one like ours.
He didn't preach; but how he prayed! God seemed right
there among us.

A regular guy; feet hard on the ground, but handfuls of
   sky to share.
He made sense out of a lot of queer things going on inside
   my mind.
Want to hear them, Buddy?
Of course, if you're bored . . .
O.K. I'll go on for a while.
This Padre didn't snivel 'round the wounded, nor shed any
   tears o'er the dead;
He didn't look pious when a guy got drunk or shot a lot
   of craps;
And he didn't " tsk, tsk " when the fellows got on a sexy
   spree.
He just threw out words, when he got a chance, in a way
   that stuck and held.
You follow me, Buddy?
No, he didn't pass out goody sweets to us; his stuff was real
   all through.
He said our bellies would drag the ground if we didn't see
   the whole of it clear and true.
He told it right when he said we could " go to hell right fast."
And he didn't miss it far when he said, " The world's right
   behind where you go."
I did a lot of thinking and kept on 'til I got it straight.
Then I didn't worry about a job,
Just got ready for the one which came.
There was no time for moping, and souring the hours to
   waste.
I decided what I wanted to do.
I got education and training, which had all been arranged. . . .
The Padre helped me to see my way into the future, as
   part of a great new world;
Cynicism I left behind.
He gave me my cue for taking stock and clicking my mind
   in that groove.

He said, "Don't be a parasite and lean on the ribbons you
wear.
Don't feel apart and let others take on your share."
The Padre said it would all make sense if we tried to be
honest and care.

You can't understand what?
Why there was a war? Why it ever started at all?
What has happened to God, who used to run the whole
show here on earth?
What sense is there in this cock-eyed world when half of
it's ruined or dead?
Come on, Buddy, put on the brakes, let's simmer down from
that boil.
I can give a few slants the Padre gave, that cut the same
kinks in my mind.
Want to hear?
Sure, I thought a lot of things out there in that messy hell;
Close grips with the Nips was filthy and grim; they were
hard to flush and kill.
Whenever I thought my number was up, I, too, cursed and
swore against God.
But it didn't help to blast the air blue, for I shook on just
the same.
Once the Chaplain heard me at it; he didn't say a word.
Just sat and looked steady at me and didn't bat an eye.
Guess he figured he couldn't say much to me then.
But later, when the Nips ceased throwing hot steel,
We batted around a thought or two, before we dropped off
exhausted to sleep.
The Padre was there. He didn't say much, but what he
said struck home.
"Men," he said quiet-like, "life here is not worth a dime
unless we've got the worth of it deep down.

" You, what you are, is the true worth; your body may be
  marked for junk."

Funny to hear him talk that way and not mind at all, but in
  it find consolation.

" God's right here — now don't you say it, for I'm telling
  you what I know, even if you don't —

" God's right here. He is life, and the stink of death can't
  make us forget.

" Yes, I know we have killed and must kill again, and that
  part of us God doesn't share — save the burden of it.

" Man's life is his all, and God is his life, and because of
  that men go on.

" Your soul is real and it doesn't die; John goes on even if
  Jones must end.

" You've got a soul, I tell you true, it is God inside that
  makes you you.

" Keep it fine; hold it high; it's all you've got."

Buddy, those men listened when they wanted to sleep,

For the Chaplain's words gave sense to their minds, and
  comfort for their souls.

He put us to sleep that night with an arrow prayer.

I remember the words of it, for they shot home and nailed
  me to strong faith in what he said.

" O God, without thee we are nothing, and this place is
  world's end; but with thee even the darkness has windows
  for the light and there is no room for fear; come near to
  each one and bless his bones, and give him rest this night.
  Amen."

How do you like it, Buddy?

That Padre, what a man!

Mind if I stretch a bit before I spin more of my yarn?

It's good to stretch and reach hands high and know you can
  move without fear.

Foxholes for foxes, say I, not men; and trenches for loath-
some rats.

I'm through hugging the earth, and crawling in muck, and
scratching lice off my flesh.

Good clean water and fresh clean " sacks " and food not out
of a can.

But let's settle again and a few things I'll tell, as far as I've
gotten myself.

That Padre out there spoke of prayer, and most peculiar
it was.

The preacher back home had not made it clear; he had said
it was " talking with God."

He didn't say how or where or when, just assumed that
I'd know, I guess.

But the Padre was honest and said quite a lot, and we believed
he was right.

" Praying," he said, " is like loading a gun, which you've
first learned all about.

" You can take it apart and put it back and know how to
aim it and shoot.

" That much you must know, but before the big show someone must furnish ammunition.

" We Johnnys have prayer guns, we know how to shoot,
but we click instead of go boom.

" It's only a click, not a bang, when we say ' there's no God,'
' oh, hell, what's the use? '

" To pray," he said, " is easy, and I'll tell you how it's done.

" But it's not prayer 'less you lean on Another and believe
you can't make it alone.

" We all believe somewhat in God, a few maybe more than
others;

" But to reach him, connect, to carry on conversation,

" We must humbly ask, and mean it, for God to show us
what's right.

" By right, we mean what is right for us as He comes into
the picture.

" But men find it hard to see Him unless they know Him
through his Son;

" That Man who made clear what God was like.

" He showed us a God we all could see;

" Could see and hear and maybe touch, and feel near in
our hearts.

" You don't need words, though words may help to keep
your mind on your praying.

" But heart and mind all primed to hear are all we need at
the start.

"A little time, a desire to find whatever He wants us to know,

" Will make it clear that He is near and soon we can load
up the barrel."

The Padre was sure wound up 'bout that time and went on
for quite a spell.

But when he got through we felt we could pray, and some
of us gave it fair trial.

If God was there, then God is here, and prayer is about
the same.

Does that help any, Buddy? We might try it now.

How about it? Let's see if it works.

No one will see. Come on, I'll show you how it's done.

Just close your eyes and sit right there, and think hard on
feeling Him near.

I'll do the same and say a few words, if any come to be said.

Concentrate will, give heart and mind, all you've got to
the task.

Forget yourself; now let God speak; keep your eyes closed;
be quiet and still. . . .

There were no words, but didn't you feel something stir
deep down inside?

Didn't things brighten up; doesn't it seem that now you can
    make the grade?
You felt it, Buddy? I knew you would. It 'most always
    works that way.
When things get dark and we face a wall, it's good to close
    your eyes;
To yearn for a glimpse of light, a way over, around or
    through.
Just a pin-prick of light, and the wall has vanished, or it
    quietly fades away;
When in my heart I've said this word, " Oh, God, I'm
    wanting to go your way."
Each time I've tried, the easier it's got, and I tell you again,
    it works;
When my desire is right and I want to know, and I'm ready
    to take it straight.

PRAYER

Since the clergyman is being called on constantly for
offering opening prayers at public gatherings, a note on in-
vocations will probably not be amiss. It is a bit dangerous
and presumptuous to leave the pattern of the prayer up to
the inspiration of the moment. Far better, it seems to me,
to prepare the invocation carefully in a quiet moment and
jot down at least the outline. I prefer to write out such
prayers verbatim and commit them to memory. We must
know what we are praying for as well as the One to whom
we pray. The following prayers were used as indicated.

For a Historical Society

O God, our help in ages past, grant us thy continuing
help and blessing, as we seek to restore and preserve the

great shrines of our native commonwealth; may our work of acquiring, restoring, and preserving the ancient relics of our country's beginnings be more than that of designating and setting apart historic grounds, buildings, monuments and tombs; may there be also preserved within each sacred place the spirit of greatness which is the real fire which kindles our remembrance. Help us, dear Father, to pass along intact to posterity the love of freedom and beauty which inspired men of yore to establish and maintain homes whence have come the lives of our ancestors. Keep us from weariness in the task, and when our own work is done, raise up strong hands and loving minds to carry on what we have begun. May the year to come be full of further signs of restoration as hopeful notes of the enduring in a world tottering among the ruins of ancient places. Be thou our guide and our wisdom as our labor is done to thy glory, through the spirit of Jesus Christ our Lord. Amen.

For the American Red Cross

Lord God of mercy, we are dedicated to thy service; may we ever keep before us the love of thy dear Son, that his spirit may walk the earth to heal and to bless; may we continue as one of the human instruments of thy compassion, and let us never become dulled or deaf to any need of thy children in this our time; may we keep close unto thee to find motive power for our deeds and make us ever mindful of our blessings of abundance, so that our greatest desire will be to share them with all who are in need, because of Jesus Christ our Lord. Amen.

For a Community Project

Dear God, we are thankful that thou hast given unto us every good and perfect gift; grant that all of our resources may be used for thy service, and that the great cause of humanity's distress may sharpen our consciences and empower our tongues; let the light of our message so shine before men that they may see it and respond to its brightness; as we have offered ourselves as messengers, so may we be filled with earnest zeal and steadfast faith, and at last present unto thee the human assurance that every need within reach of our ability has been provided for. We ask for thy blessing and direction, and that all of our work begun in thy name may be furthered and ended in the same, through the Spirit of Christ. Amen.

For an Education Association

Dear God and Father of all mankind, we ask thy power and strength for a more effectual communication of our faith in thee to those with whom we live; help us to acknowledge our faith in thee by the facing of every difficulty unafraid, and the facing of every perplexity dependent upon thy guidance for the right and best choice; may the light of thy presence shine through our minds and through all our deeds, that a portion of thy glory may be seen in us; enlighten with thy wisdom those of us who teach and those who come to us and would learn; help us to fill every hungry heart and every seeking mind, and let not lesser matters concern us and blind us to the greater; make us strong to serve thee faithfully in the days to come, that wherever we are and whatever we do, " there shall be no night there " because within us thy spirit dwells secure in the love of Jesus Christ our Lord. Amen.

CHAPTER VI

ADDRESSES AND MAGAZINE ARTICLES

Write the vision, and make it plain upon tables,
that he may run that readeth it.

HABAKKUK 2:2

ALL CLERGYMEN will be called on at some time in their ministry to give a lecture and to write a paper or an article for a magazine. This demands time for research and careful preparation. And woe unto any clergyman who throws together his material and trusts to the inspiration of the moment to see him through. The word " drool " is not a good one according to the English professor's standard, but it is an apt description of some lectures from my brethren, and alas, my own attempts have too often fitted this category. God's word requires labor to gather and form and transmit to others. Unless we can do a good job, it is better to decline, and let someone else do the work, admitting that we are too busy with our many activities to closet ourselves long enough to create flesh for the bones assigned to us.

All but the last of the following examples were written to be read, and then published. The second and third, which I called at first " My Four Months in a Mental Hospital " and " Look to Your Preaching," were delivered and revised several times before appearing in print. Almost every time one's writing is revised it is improved. Incidentally (but quite necessary for me) my wife is my writing team mate. We work like this: I write, she corrects and suggests; I rewrite, she checks over it again; I polish. This procedure is followed, when time permits, before each use of the material.

Take the Kinks Out of Parsons!

It might seem the height of temerity for me, an imperfect parson, even to mention the need for ironing kinks out of some of the clergy, myself included. But this problem is of tragic importance. We are headed for a postwar era of endless and exacting demands upon Christian clergymen. We cannot afford to enter such a period handicapped by the halt and the blind, the lame and the bigoted among us. We are potential leaders toward the new world of community power, with its appalling perplexities and problems, demanding our best.

I am now rapidly becoming an old boy and as I travel back over the years, there is a heavy burden of sadness because of the ministry that might have been if my kinks had begun to be ironed out sooner. As I preach in various places and keep my eyes and ears open, I see many obvious kinks that could easily be corrected and yet are not; indeed many of the clergymen who have one or more of these outward and visible signs of inner need are not even aware of it. But the ministries of these men are frequently ruined by this blindness — and in consequence there is no effective witness for Christ.

One Lent, during a particularly revealing evening, I caught a vision of a " kinks-out " school for clergy, where, in clinic fashion, the problems of clergymen could be correctly diagnosed and their habits and lives changed to the greater glory of God and the advancement of their calling. This would take humility galore on the part of the parson to be " de-kinked," and some marvelous Christian understanding, love, and tact on the part of the presiding elder, bishop, or whoever might be the immediate authority responsible for the conduct becoming every minister under him. Or it might well be a friend who would open eyes and guide the faulty one.

Let me reminisce awhile over some of the kinks I have actually seen (including a few of my own I have discovered and am in the process of dealing with) and then let me paint a picture of such a proposed clinic.

One of our best guides to the discovery of the kinks is a Litany [1] designed by an English bishop to offer up all the faults of his clergy for God to remove, of course with the utmost co-operation of the clergymen. I list them in order of their appearance (with a few scattered ones of my own). Note his penetrating insight, from first-hand experience, no doubt, of the frailties to which the holy brotherhood is heir. Check down the list. Where it hurts a bit place a mark. Add the marks up later to reveal the need.

(1) Annoying, distracting, and unpleasant mannerisms; flaws in voice placement, quality, and diction. (2) Eccentricities of dress. (3) Family life contrary to the ideal people have a right to expect. (4) Carelessness in the use of money — one's own and that belonging to the church. (5) Blindness to propriety. (6) Ineffective presentation of the good news of Christ. (7) Moral weakness, timidity, hesitation, fear of men, dread of responsibility. (8) Weakness of judgment, indecision, irresolution, loss of opportunities. (9) Infirmity of purpose, want of earnest care and interest, the sluggishness of indolence, the slackness of indifference, spiritual deadness. (10) Dullness of conscience, feeble sense of duty, thoughtless disregard of consequences, half-heartedness. (11) Weariness in continuing struggles, despondency in failure and disappointment, overburdened sense of unworthiness, morbid fancies, imaginary backslidings. (12)

---

[1] From *The Southwell Litany*. The Forward Movement. Used by permission.

Self-conceit, vanity, boasting, delight in supposed success and superiority, offensive manners, self-assertion. (13) Affectation, untruth, pretense, impulsive self-adaptation in endeavor to please, false appearances. (14) Love of flattery, over-ready belief in praise, dislike of criticism, comfort of self-deception. (15) Love of display, sacrifice to popularity, thought of self in forgetfulness of God, self-glorification. (16) Pride, self-will, desire to have one's own way, over-weening love of one's own ideas, blindness to the value of others, resentment against opposition, contempt for the claims of others, selfish arbitrariness of temper. (17) Jealousy, grudging other's success, impatience of submission, eagerness for authority, insubordination to law, order, and authority. (18) Hasty utterances of impatience, retort of irritation, taunt of sarcasm, infirmity of temper in provoking or being provoked, love of unkind gossip, idle words that may hurt. (19) Stubborn rejection of new revelations. (20) Arrogance in our dealings with all men. (21) Fancies, delusions, prejudices of habit. (22) False judgments, misplaced trust and distrust, misplaced giving and refusing, misplaced praise and rebuke.

When we consult our ordination vows again, we are aghast at the great gulf we have allowed to appear between the life we've lived and the demand " until ye have done all that lieth in you." What can be done, then, for the brethren who are as yet blind and who, for Christ's sake, must be given sight? A loving friend *could* do a lot — perhaps a wife, or older fellow clergyman whom we respect and admire and love. But there are too few persons like Ananias to minister to needy Sauls — to give sight to the blind and light to them that walk in darkness. Therefore some central house or school or clinic must be provided where the church will place experts to unravel and de-kink, to give second birth to, in short, renew life and lift it to its maximum usefulness.

There would be financial experts to teach us how to live on a budget and to keep bills paid and to give some real business sense to the — as a rule — financially inexpert cleric. There would be voice experts to iron out the faulty use of the voice (such as swallowing words, speaking with a nasal quality, using wrong emphases and monotony of tone); and unpleasant mannerisms (such as pulling the nose, walking around in the pulpit, and aimless movements of hands and arms). There would be literary experts to check on style and form of sermons, articles, and letters. There would be promotion experts to help with the problem of conducting successful money-raising campaigns, to instruct in the use of effective newspaper publicity, the value of good printing, and other aids for making a parish known.

There would be expert psychologists to iron out phobias, anti-social attitudes, personality queerness, quirks, depressions, minor persecution complexes, projections, and the like. There would be personnel experts to show how to handle people and deal with them intelligently. There would be expert theologians to check and clarify ideas and beliefs and presentation of the great truths of the Christian religion. There would be expert social case workers to help work out records and plans for dealing with pastoral problems; expert administrators to help in running the complicated organizational life of a parish.

But, finally, and most important, there would be experts in the devotional life — spiritual pastors, soul doctors — who would help to clean up the clergyman's personal life and to unclog the channels of the Spirit. In this area we find the greatest need — the need to know the Shepherd as well as his song. There is widespread blindness to one's own spiritual needs. We are too often concerned with Bible reading, prayer, and sermons for others without due regard for the growth of our own Christian selves.

65p39.

Why could not all of this be done in seminary? Because most of our kinks do not develop until we are out on our own; besides, we have few opportunities to uncover those that already exist until some time has been spent in the pastoral ministry. How would men find their way to the clinic? The presiding elder or bishop, or another in authority, would normally see or sense the kinks and suggest a trip to the clinic, paying the expenses if necessary, writing to the clinic whatever information will help in the ironing-out process.

This idea may be good, but if no one cares enough to recognize the need and work out some such cure, we may be found wanting at war's end and have on our hands a bunch of empty, solemn ministers, not worthy of the name "pastor." As Phillips Brooks put it: " with their straight coats of precision, like a chest of drawers which Bob Sawyer showed to Mr. Winkle in his little surgery, ' Dummies,' my dear boy, ' half the drawers have nothing in them, and the other half don't open.' " Instead of this kind of clergymen we must have balanced Spirit-filled men of power.

We are called of God to live our utmost and to be his channels for earth blessedness.

Ministers and Strait Jackets

I spent four months of my life in a mental hospital. The summer of 1931 between terms at the seminary I went to the Worcester State Hospital in Worcester, Massachusetts — not as a patient, but as one to whom the hospital had much to give. I realized that, even then. Worcester was chosen because of its progressive work along therapeutic lines for the mentally sick. It is the oldest of the many state hospitals in Massachusetts. This hospital was, at the time, in the midst of many new experiments which gave promise of results in cures. I remember well the work of Doctor Marsh and his approach to group therapy (we called them Marsh prayer meetings), the work of some French doctor in the realm of hypnosis, the use of radio and music in an experimental way, and many other methods and drugs that gave promise of cure or relief to the mentally sick — all of these were being used at the time of my stay there.

I had become absorbed in psychology and psychiatry and social case work while at the seminary and was convinced that in these fields lay the answer to a successful pastoral ministry, which quite naturally I wanted to achieve. I learned later that it took a lot more than mere desire.

At the hospital I worked in the wards as attendant five hours a day, with one day off each week; for another five hours I attended lectures, studied case records, talked with patients, worked on the two case histories which were to be required as proof of my learning. There were many extra-curricular activities in the evenings and at odd hours in the laboratories, wards, operating and autopsy rooms; and much time was spent in comparing notes with others there — young interns, occupational therapy workers, nurses, and embryo preachers. It was the most expanding and expansive period of my life up to that point and made an impression I have never forgotten.

As I think back, I believe I went there primarily to learn about sick minds as a clue to sick souls, and to understand as much of the cause and the cure as possible. Spinoza gave me the words for it, " Human actions should not be laughed at, should not be shocked at, nor held in disdain, but should be understood." During my stay at Worcester I did learn a bit about how to understand the mental mechanism of both abnormal and normal human beings, and this has been of inestimable help to me in my ministry. The greatest benefits came from a better understanding of the " peculiar " individuals one meets every day outside mental hospitals — also of myself. I can still see moving in front of me the infinite tragedy of sorrow and suffering both in families and individuals, as well as that tremendously valuable thing called the human personality, which the hospital was trying to save; I can also see through the windows of my experience these same human situations outside hospitals, likewise going through, as it were, their daily performance. Such insights have enabled me to approach a bit nearer to my ideal: have given me the ability to enter into the hearts and minds of others, to understand. I believe I have been a better priest, an infinitely better pastor, and a more understanding husband and father for having seen humanity in the raw, and for having glimpsed a few causes of the rawness and the success of a few cures.

Carroll A. Wise, then Assistant Chaplain of Worcester State Hospital, with whom I worked during that summer, has written a valuable book on *Religion in Illness and Health*. It covers the subject of religion at work in a mental hospital and the clergyman's part in the co-operative work of doctor, psychiatrist, and pastor, in dealing with the intricate and interrelated workings of man's life — body, mind, soul, and spirit. This book is good for those who work in hospitals and for those who work outside.

During my limited experience with mental illness that summer, I was able to reach several conclusions which still seem valid, conclusions about the processes of the human mind, the start of such processes and the end. These conclusions were based upon a wide reading and firsthand contact with every known form of mental disease, both functional and organic, among the twenty-five hundred patients in the hospital. These diseases ranged from general paresis, through schizophrenia and paranoia types, to the wastebasket of mental diagnosis — the psycopathic personality. I realized that the organic group was beyond my ken and so concentrated mainly on the functional group, especially that difficult wastebasket group which is made up of individuals who are so normal most of the time that very few of them ever go to mental hospitals, but who come frequently into the pastor's study during one of their "queer" periods. My interest, then, had to do with the functional psychoses — that is, those not based upon any organic causation or lesion.

My first conclusion was that the fundamental cause of most of these functional psychoses was some kind of inner conflict, as yet unresolved. The inability to make a decision or to take a stand keeps one's mind and spirit in a state of tension and turmoil, and this leads eventually (unless terminated in some other way) to an attempted escape through living in another world (schizophrenia), or to a complex of some kind (paranoic-persecution), or into a depression (manic-depressive). A sense of guilt, a feeling of fear, aroused anger, a frustration or repression, the primitive instincts and passions, and appetites such as sex and hunger, are in the forefront as causes of these psychoses and neuroses.

Knowing the results and the things that lead to them enables one who is alert enough and trained a bit to detect signs far enough in advance to shunt them off from the otherwise inevitable consequences. This has enabled me to sometimes catch heart and soul sickness before it becomes mind sickness. I try to keep a sharp lookout for the first signs of lack of control in attitudes and tendencies, and on discovering them, I try to help relax and resolve the various factors of tension and conflicts involved, so as to redirect and control the dangerous tendencies. I learned that my job as pastor is not to attempt to be a psychiatrist but a Christian psychologist, who will show how the past may be purged of its fears and stings and bitter hurts, and so point the way to release from the bondage of the past. Pastors must deal with present conditions in individuals which, if left alone, may lead to mental sickness, from uncontrolled anger to obsessions of persecution or inferiority or guilt — when persons so afflicted are willing to yield up these evil pets. My experience has helped me to distinguish between neuroses and psychoses, and personality kinks and maladjustments, to see that the former cases are sent to a psychiatrist, and the latter are dealt with in a thorough, intelligent, spiritual fashion, often in co-operation with a doctor. My experience has helped me to deal with borderline cases and to keep those who could be helped from continuing their journey in the dark toward deeper darkness.

If for no other reason, then, I am thankful for this experience, for it has prevented me from belonging to that certain group of clergymen who, having read a few books on moral theology, psychology, and social case work, strive to combine the methods in use in the various fields into a *vade mecum* for their pastoral ministry. Unfortunately, most of these men are dabblers, feeling and attempting to act like experts after having read a single book, perhaps in each field; and the results of their advice frequently reveal their amateurish standing, to say nothing of the actual harm done. The chief blunders we clergymen sometimes make, tragic to souls in need, come from conclusions based upon the principles and techniques of a science about which we know little or nothing. In so doing we lose the respect of the experts in these fields. Of course, we must read books, attend lectures and conferences to broaden and increase our knowledge of human nature and human relations. But we must not in the name of honesty and decency pose as experts until we have expertly mastered one field, and have proven our ability to practice in that field. My own hospital experience quite definitely prevented me ever after from posing as an expert. I remember a quotation from Hippocrates garnered that summer from a lecture: "To know is one thing; merely to believe one knows is another. To know is science, but merely to believe one knows is ignorance."

The trend of the Christian religion today is toward more co-operation with medical science, psychology, and psychiatry especially, and its exact and exacting approach toward people's difficulties (*The Soul Doctor*, by Doctor Zahnizer, explains it well). The trend of modern psychiatry is toward an understanding of the whole man, recognizing the many hidden factors with which the Christian religion can deal, such as faith for fear, forgiveness for guilt. A well-known psychiatrist informs me that rarely do we find a meeting of psychiatrists today where the soul or spirit or total personality and being of man are not considered seriously and at length. Therefore, it is important that the clergy and the medical profession work more closely together as allies in the quest for preventives and cures for the minds and souls of men.

I have since worked with several doctors and psychiatrists on functional cases, and have recently had a distinguished psychiatrist, Dr. Gregory Zilborg, speak in my chapel on *The Smiling Christ*. I shall not soon forget the first case I had of such co-operation after leaving the hospital that summer. A certain doctor had reached the end of his rope with a patient and in desperation called me in as a minister. The patient was in a deep depression caused by a horrible sense of sin and guilt, and was a potential suicide; the doctor realized that a sense of forgiveness was the only thing which could save him. We battled for hours without success. The man did commit suicide. This was a blow to my pride and my conscience. What could have saved him? This case and others made me realize the need for more than a knowledge of mental states and case records, and convinced me that the love and power of God must also be accepted as present or no cure. The inadequacies of psychiatry for the whole man became clear to me then and I have not forgotten.

Certain experiences in the hospital and other experiences since have kept me in remembrance of most of the things learned while there. I well remember my initial trip through the wards; the terrible and vivid impression of that first glimpse never grew commonplace. I never became a hardened witness to this world of locks and keys and paced longings, for which there was so often no fulfillment; this land of the dead whose only hope lay in a resurrection; this winding, tortuous, heart-rending lane of living rooms, each wrapping within itself a tragedy — beings whose last vestige of the human seemed for the moment to have been torn away — disgusting, repulsive, yet so very pitiful. I thought, this pile of stone is a progressive mental hospital, stemming from the cruel days of custodial care only — an asylum full to the brim with the sick, and is dedicated wholly to their care and cure.

My first impression was of deadly monotony, a routine of idleness and brooding. This impression was soon corrected, however, by the many bright spots — the never-flagging zeal, interest, and kindness of the doctors, nurses, and attendants. They went at their task of releasing each patient from his own little hell with the contagious assurance that it could be done.

When those outside realize that mental illness is the result of the normal processes of life becoming for the moment top-heavy and unbalanced, and not the just punishment for some sin, nor the manifestation of an evil infestation, the chances for a person's return to normal life will be greatly enhanced. None of us is immune. I found there a college professor whose self-centered, selfish sex life got out of control; a young Roman Catholic priest troubled with an over-

powering sense of inferiority; a doctor, a lawyer, a business-
man falling before the inevitable results of neglected syphilis;
a laborer whose thirsty lips were cooled too often; a woman
deprived of her share of love; a young girl paying the price
of "happy" hours; a child who had never learned to play.
Most of them, if they had known, could have been helped
back to health before the break came.

The best way to study a subject is to battle your way to
its source. That is what I tried to do. Through case studies
and actual contact with their living counterparts, the ignorance of gigantic pictures conjured up by such words as
"schizophrenia" and "paranoia" were made clear and
sharply defined — the fearsome unattainable became a commonplace. I repeat: the key word to the understanding of
all mental illness is "conflict." Conflicts usually arise from
threats and fears, from the rebellion of suppressed feelings,
and from things we do not want to know and will not face.
When we find out what causes the conflict, we can usually
find a cure. When a person is adjusted *to* and *for* life, with
an absorbing interest at heart, he rarely ever goes "haywire."

Our radio studio at the hospital was an attic room, all
bright with gunnysacks and squeaky chairs, a silent window,
a baby piano and a tiny mike. We found that the patients
actually did enjoy our sparkling programs of musical hi-
larity! I was Little Merry Sunshine and broadcast a fifteen-
minute program of music and good advice each morning.
Over this hospital radio we practiced group hypnosis for the
quieting of patients in the pack rooms, and they needed it.
We also broadcast special musical programs to calm and
orient certain types of illness. None of these experiments
was conclusive. Here, I suppose, I got my first thought of
a "Haven" — later my daily, early morning devotional
program of five minutes.

My favorite patient was Sarah Cottrell — Sadie, a psychoneurotic whose case I studied in endless detail. We became great friends. I shall give a brief résumé of part of her story.

I remember days and nights with Sadie, bat after bat, one day groggy with paraldehyde, the next doped and crazy, the next moody and threatening. Many a time in camisole (strait jacket), many a night of moans and bad dreams. I learned to handle Sadie both physically and mentally. She would not fight me. I carried her back from many a crazed wandering in a maze of wards. I tried to be a real friend.

I sat by her bedside at night, watching her sunken lips utter words and emit the stench of paraldehyde. I assisted in putting her in sheet restraint after mad struggles, with Margaret, her shadow-light, the good ghost of a bad memory, always hovering in the background. " Things " crawled on the wall for Sadie, pictures turned to demons, horrors! I remember when for over a week Sadie was at her worst. Then one morning she awoke weak, terribly weak, but normal. She gradually made a comeback. Her powers of recuperation were amazing. I told her all that had happened. She remembered nothing. She was heartbroken to learn of her condition. After this, when I inquired how she was, her answer was invariably, " Oh, not too bad! "

I read to her much of the time. She was still weak and had to stay in bed. In addition to this lamentable mental condition, she had tuberculosis. One lung was gone and the other looked like a snowstorm in the X-rays. She smoked innumerable cigarettes. How could they deprive her? She had been " sentenced " already. She told me tales of her life in Canada, hair-raising stories of her existence in the mental hospitals there. She had the reputation of being the worst patient in the history of the hospital on Prince Edward Island. I shall never forget her telling of this incident.

The pathetic first night in a mental hospital. Alone with strange noises, a terrible stench, and the horrible fear of death. She was fretting so much they put her in a camisole by force and locked her in, to sleep as best she could. This was the first link in Sadie's rebellion against attendants and nurses and doctors — a rebellion which has not abated to this day. She decided to meet cruelty with resistance. As a result, she stayed in camisole most of the time under lock and key. There were many, many such tales.

Sadie was allowed parole as soon as she was better, and we had long walks together. She loved the quiet and peace of the woods. It was her church, her confessional. Favorite spots became shrines. I could never help her much, but she did unburden herself to me. At such times she thought clearly and deeply upon the vital issues of her life as contrasted with others more fortunate than she. Sometimes she became a bit bitter. At other times, she was quite cheerful and often said: " God is good. It is his will." She wanted to be a good Catholic. Sadie was always kind when she was in her right mind. It is hard to leave the story of Sadie. Incident after incident crowd into my mind out of the past, but leave her we must.

I grew in patience and compassion. Such words as integration, insight, maturity, became intelligible. The common sources of conflict stood out as unbridled appetites (usually sex), violent emotions (fear and anger); and the major sins, according to psychology, were learned to be fear and anger. Jesus dealt with them, and in the Sermon on the Mount are adequate answers.

I learned also:

That tension is commonly associated with three emotions: anxiety, guilt, and resentment;

That hatred and resentment, guilt and shame and anxiety produce conflict and frustration;

That unsolved personal problems in one period of life are always a handicap in the next period;

That the " I " and not the " Thou " is at the center of all functional psychoses and incipient mental sickness;

That one does not break the laws of the inner or of the external world without suffering;

That adaptation to environment is essential for mental health — adaptation to new and difficult situations;

That to have inner adjustment to life, real spiritual control of life — poise and tranquillity of mind — is to be mentally healthy;

That insight and faith concerning the unknown (this really includes all the problems of life and therefore the higher levels of growth) is the heart of religion;

That true religion leads the individual to a way of life based on the principles of insight and co-operation, not on those of evasion and escape;

That Jesus had the perfect grasp of realities and insights that lead to wholeness. God's laws must be obeyed or. . . .

As I grow older I am ever more grateful for this view into the mental illnesses of men and the importance of mental hygiene, which is in reality the importance of religion in the normal and abnormal life of man.

This phase of my pastoral training gave new meaning to that later occasion when I took my ordination vows. I have often thought of one of them. I can hear the Bishop saying now: ". . . and see that ye never cease your labor, your care and diligence, until ye have done all that lieth in you . . . to bring all such as are or shall be committed to your charge into the agreement in the faith and knowledge of God, and to that ripeness and perfectness of age in Christ, that there be no place left among you, either for error in religion, or for viciousness in life." [1]

To which then, and now, I am willing to respond, " I will."

[1] From "Service of Ordination to the Priesthood," in *The Book of Common Prayer*. Church Pension Fund. Used by permission.

In Unknown Tongues

Brethren, I speak to you now about sermons. Recent experiences with sermons and sermonizing, all the way from the bare-bones kind to the inspired-utterance kind, have sharpened my wit concerning them; and from these same experiences (much of them concerned with my own homiletical need) I have gained the convictions which follow. I speak from the viewpoint of our common affliction — "sinners" in search of a better way.

Sermons, for many laymen (so they tell me about some of my own), are utterances by ministers in unknown tongues, unknown to both speaker and listener; and, they say, what follows a text seems to fulfill the promise of Paul in 1 Corinthians 15:51: "Behold, I shew you a mystery." Of course, Paul was not talking about sermons, and I am not talking about all sermons, only those which mystify and do not reveal.

The words found in 1 Thessalonians must be the end and aim of our search: " For our preaching of the good news did not come to you as mere words, but with power and the holy Spirit and full conviction. . . . For our appeal does not rest on a delusion, nor spring from any impure motive; there is no fraud about it. God has thought us fit to be intrusted with the good news, and so we tell it, making no effort to please men, but to please God, who tests our hearts." (1 Thessalonians 1:5; 2:3, 4)[1]

Whatever words I may say will have as their fundamental purpose and objective the bringing to the fore of a few essential thoughts on how to make a sermon speak, in the vernacular, the understandable and wonder-working words of God in all their beauty and power; and to suggest how to

---

[1] From *The Bible, An American Translation*, by Smith and Goodspeed. Used by permission of the University of Chicago Press.

create in those who listen a willingness of expectation. "The miracle of preaching" need not be the lost art of a skeptical age.

I

Our first thought is stirred into life by these words of L. W. Grensted, from his vivid and masterful book *The Person of Christ*. "We (must) speak of that we know and testify of that we have seen. Only so is there any hope that men will receive our witness." Each pulpit ascent must be made to the rhythm of whispered words never to be forgotten — "speak a good word for the Lord Jesus." [1]

A gold mine of sermon technique that shook the very souls of those who heard is to be found in the Acts of the Apostles. Here we find brief summary sermons — the Christian religion in gist — with vitality and convincing power. Here we find illustrated that witness Grensted mentions and that remembered word, "Speak a good word for the Lord Jesus."

The significance of Peter's first sermon, for instance, in Acts 2:14-39, lies not in its literary excellence, nor in its tie-up of present with past, nor in its poignant picture of Jesus, but rather in its bold declaration of truth about man's share in the crucifixion of Jesus whom God declared to be both Lord and Savior. By simplicity and honesty Peter convicted the people and won them to an immediate desire to do something about this sense of guilt. "When they heard this, they were stung to the heart." Peter in turn, without verbiage or stalling, told them explicitly to repent, be baptized, and receive forgiveness of sins and the gift of the Holy Spirit, which they in turn could share with both family and friends.

[1] From *The Person of Christ*, by L. W. Grensted. Harper & Brothers, publishers. Used by permission.

Would it not have a salutary effect on preachers today if members of the congregation were encouraged to fire questions — such as a " Why? " here and a " How? " there, and " What have you found from personal experience? " or " Is this your own opinion? " — and to seize and act upon moments of inspiration as they come? Sermons should lift people out of their seats and start their desires, and later their footsteps, in the direction of the pastor's study for further, personalized details.

Peter knew from his own personal experience the Way he advocated for others. There are no high-sounding words nor mystifying phrases, nor attempts to compromise in this first sermon of Peter's; and, while it might not be considered perfect in a homiletics class, the record bears witness to the fact that it changed the lives of three thousand people on the spot. To say that hardly three understood or were touched might well describe the aftermath of thousands of Sunday sermons today. The power of Peter's word was inner and spiritual. Herein is the answer to " How could it happen? " — his heart and mind were in tune with God's will and way.

2

We must not forget, either, that Peter's sermon was short! So were all of the sermons recorded in the Acts. It did not take these pioneer preachers long to do the job. As we look at their sermons, we find tucked away in nearly every one of them something specific about the technique of forgiveness and fellowship with Christ. Note as another example the second sermon of Peter's in Acts 3:12-26, or his sermonette in Acts 4:8-12. There is no mincing of words in either of them. In a few clear sentences, he enunciates the good news.

Take another incident of preaching in Acts 7:2-53. Young Stephen is the preacher. Stephen's sermon is longer and more involved, but it, too, eventually gets down to basic principles. And yet Stephen's greater witness followed the sermon and undoubtedly did more good than the sermon itself: he practiced what he preached and people knew it. Strange how quickly we ourselves forget the content of what we preach. Many of us would be hard put to recall on a Sunday night, even in summary fashion, the " masterpiece " of the morning, much less to practice it explicitly.

At a clerical meeting recently the program committee arranged for a surprise program. There were sixteen clergymen present. The subject was announced: " Each one must give the text, the aim, and the gist of yesterday's sermon " — remember this was only one day after it was preached. Only the three on the committee did an adequate job, and even two of these fell down a bit on the aim part. All of the others muddled, and could not give in a sentence or two just what they had tried to do the day before. Pathetic? Yes, but all too typical. Had Peter been in the group, he could have told exactly what he had said because he always kept to the fundamentals of his own beliefs and experiences. I must always admit, when I am pinned down to it, that my own sermons suffer frequently from lack of clarity of aim and concreteness of purpose, which I seem never to remedy completely.

3

Another secret of these early sermons in the Acts is that they were preached under the direction of the Holy Spirit. The results prove this. It was a kind of preaching in which self was entirely forgotten. Jesus only was central. They had no inhibitions, therefore, concerning what might happen to them or what people might think of them. Only one thing mattered — for men to repent and accept Christ. Too often our words are controlled by what people may think of us personally or what consequences may follow some words too boldly uttered. When such a condition as this exists, it is high time for the guilty one to cry, " Get thee behind me, Satan."

Another of Peter's sermons, preached this time to Cornelius and his household, is a masterpiece on race relations — he proved there are no race problems when Christ comes into one's life. Never forget that the power of this sermon came because Peter, only at long last, was freed from his own race prejudices and openly admitted that " God . . . taught (him) not to call anyone vulgar or unclean," and that " God shows no partiality." (Acts 10:28b, 35)[1]

Paul's sermons, which come to the fore in the last half of the Acts, are similar in outline and content to Peter's, but there is the addition of several great new themes, such as the one which he enunciates in his sermon at Pisidian Antioch, the famous justification by faith theme. However, Jesus and his death and resurrection and freedom from sin occupy the central emphases.

Paul's only departure from his usual method was at Athens, where he failed to win the intellectuals when he stooped to their level and tried to be something other than his real self. There was no ring of conviction and urgency to his message there, and the philosophers were left cold.

We do not have space enough for a detailed analysis of all the sermons in Acts. My point is that therein are models of perfection on the contents and results of sermons, which we must not overlook in our own preaching. " Reality " is a word we all need to remember; we find this quality uppermost in these great sermons of the early church.

In my " pre-conversion " days in the ministry, I preached largely from books and the experience of others and won-

---

[1] From *The Bible, An American Translation*, by Smith and Goodspeed. Used by permission of the University of Chicago Press.

dered why my psychology and social-service approach did not affect more people. Later I realized there was no reality and sincerity in what I said. Beauty perhaps, and literary excellence, possibly, but no reality that warmed men's hearts into spiritual growing. I, the preacher, was left blind to my own shortcomings, inconsistencies, and needs. I discovered that enthusiasm (of which there was an abundance) is no adequate substitute for truth and careful preparation; and that a thousand fine words of what John Doe thinks can never be quite so effective as two words from the preacher that ring true. From these sermons in Acts we can formulate a maxim: Sermons should stab the soul awake and not just tickle the mind without disturbing its complacent inertness.

4

Why do we preach? What is the aim, the intent of our preaching? This depends largely upon the preacher and his latent or developed ability. I think immediately of four contrasting types of preachers. The first is the excellent preacher with a wide reputation, who labors for perfection. His style is beautiful, his illustrations are apt and to the point; and his congregation sings his praises far and wide. But no one seems to be made any different by his sermons; there are very few if any conversions.

The second is the poor, unimaginative, uncreative preacher who throws together a few ideas from books or magazines or sermons recently read, and who barely manages to " get through " another Sunday. Nothing happens to those who listen to him because his words and thoughts are not his own and do not persuade or convince, no matter how good they may have been in their original context.

The third preaches sermons that glow with simple virtue and loveliness. They are poetical and they lift men up, but people wonder afterward what tangible, applicable truth he uttered. Such sermons are soon spent and the people who have heard feel " cheated," for when they try to chew the meat they think they have taken, it turns out to be a cobweb.

Then there is the fourth type, the vigorous, convicting man of God, who speaks the truth in honesty and love, who makes Jesus real and never fails to speak the good word for him, who makes God's way alluring and possible for all who hear. Men leave his services strangely changed and are no longer content to remain on any level but their highest. He never scolds, but encourages, inspires, opens doors. He is a disciple of this reality we have mentioned, and passes along what he has found for himself.

It is a marvelous feeling to know God has used your voice; and no one needs to tell us when God has used us. Then it is that the angels sing and we are wondrously happy. But too often all we can say after our preachment is that the gargoyles leered today.

5

At the root of much sermonic difficulty is " absenteeism." That is, words and thoughts are omitted, leaving blank spaces in meaning which the listeners cannot fill in. You have seen pictures in which one or more blanks indicate absent workmen or idle machines, making for inefficient production. The same effect is produced when a word used by the preacher is totally unfamiliar. Some peculiar super-ego complex makes some of us go out of our way to find and use complicated or unusual words without stopping to make them clear to our listeners. Even though this may engender feelings of " greatness " in the one who utters them, confusion follows for those who listen. At the root of this difficulty of course is the fact that such preachers are still somewhat " self-centered " rather than wholly " Christ-centered."

Another difficulty comes when ideas are bunched so succinctly that another one comes along before the one before has had time to soak in. As a result no idea remains, and the total effect is too often a blur of vagueness. One of the most fascinating of studies is etymology, the running of words back to their root or original meanings. When we break them down into their component parts, they fall to pieces and are quite easily assimilated, digested, and remembered. Our sermons should be similarly treated.

Wives can be a great help in keeping their preacher-husbands pinned down to concreteness and simplicity, and held up to vision and inspiration. Poor souls, these wives of preachers! Their job is thankless and dreary, and many preachers cannot " take " their invaluable criticism. However, we should all strive for enough Christian magnanimity to accept and use the suggestions our " best friends " give to us.

6

The value of sermons boils down to what we who preach have to say and the way we say it; and what they who listen come to get and the way they come. It is a shame that at certain times each year the situation could not be reversed in every congregation, that is, the preacher listen and one or more of the listeners preach. It would make both of them more charitable and humble and better able to discern the word of God rightly spoken. One preacher has done something similar to this. On one Sunday he published the subject, text, and outline of the following Sunday's sermon and urged the people to write their own sermons. They were supposed to bring their completed sermons with them and compare notes with the preacher's treatment of the subject.

Never before have there been so many real opportunities and needs to be seized and met through sermons. Biblical material is rich and varied and can be lifted section by section and quoted as a message for this or any time of stress and turmoil. Those who yearn to prophesy — and the need is great for those whom God allows to stand on tiptoe and see just a little farther than the rest of us — must prophesy, and their message will be almost identical with that of Jeremiah, Amos, Hosea, and many of the other prophets. All of the gloom of these prophets can be carried over into these long and sad years with the emphasis placed upon destruction and suffering as the consequences of disobedience to God's laws, and the hope of it all can be placed upon the possible reconstruction of the world on a different basis.

Ezra and Nehemiah strike the right note for us on this theme of rebuilding. Who but the preacher has the best opportunity to guide the thinking and the planning, to arouse the desire for a new and better world? His voice can be the powerhouse of a new age, presenting the truth and interpreting it so that his people will believe John's words as true: " The light is still shining in the darkness, for the darkness has never put it out." (John 1:5)[1] People are confused and insecure. They want definite answers and a concrete presentation of hope. We must deal specifically and practically with the problems of the day. We must show as clearly as we can why the innocent must suffer, so long as men make wrong choices, and why evil seems to be dominant over good, and why we can pray effectively only in harmony with God's laws, and how we can reconcile a " good God " of love with the brutal bloody business of war and its aftermath.

Yes, the canvas is large and the problems innumerable.

[1] From *The Bible, An American Translation,* by Smith and Goodspeed. Used by permission of the University of Chicago Press.

We must be about the serious and inescapable business of throwing new light on the old truth and to show how it is still possible to hope on and believe on, and finally to win some semblance of God's kingdom on earth. This is what we must preach.

And the way we preach it is of the utmost importance. We must speak with the authority of our convictions and must make it clear that this is where we stand. We cannot pussy-foot with generalities and do the job. We must give evidence of a secure and abiding faith that knows no fear, of a real love that knows no hate, and of a patience that gives endlessly to those who take overlong to understand and to accept God's way. The tongue is a powerful instrument and can calm or disturb, inspire or depress, encourage or leave cold. When our own faith is carefully wrought out on the anvil of private prayer, and when our dependence for words and thoughts is totally upon God, our congregations will be blessed indeed, and our churches will send forth the challenge that will win men to a hearing of the message of Jesus Christ.

7

But preachers waste words and beat the air unless their words find lodgment and response. Therefore we turn to the listeners. Since the essence of worship is response to God, the essence of sermons is the response of the listeners. A large per cent of each group of listeners speaks a different language from the preacher. They hear but do not understand. Therefore they leave unheeding. A small per cent hear and understand, and appreciate and declare " that was a wonderful sermon," but they never get around to demonstrating its possibilities. The remaining few leave the house of God all bright and beautiful within, for they have been touched and changed. These will carry the message into the thoughts and acts of the week. Someone has said there are three kinds of sermon listeners: The first one hears and tells the preacher how fine it was. The second one hears and tells others how truly great it was. The third tells no one perhaps, but goes and lives the implications of the sermon he has heard.

Only those who are hungry really seek for food. Jesus rightly said that those are blessed who are aware of their spiritual poverty and hunger, for they will grow rich and be fed. So long as a person is satisfied with little, he will not seek for much. That is why it is sinful to preach sermons that do not disturb and arouse. There should be a loving but stinging uppercut in sermons, to shake the listeners loose from their self-satisfied condition, their spiritual lethargy, their half-awakened intellect, their blind and unwarmed hearts. Only so will needs be seen, convictions become real, and the lives of people be fundamentally changed.

Preaching is no cure-all. It is no escape from personal contact and individual counseling. It is no ivory tower from which everything is broadcast without contact of person. Human needs must be grappled with individually. Nothing quite so simple as writing a sermon will answer completely. So sermons, as a rule, have not done their work until the carpet on the pastor's study floor is worn smooth by many feet, and his hours for appointment are crowded daily.

CHAPTER VII

THE USE OF DRAMA

Every man heard them speak in his own language.
ACTS 2:6

VERY FEW CLERGYMEN claim talent in the area of the dramatic, although the annual Christmas and Easter pageants often find them in the harrowing role of script writer, entrepreneur, electrician, director, costumer, and "voice." Such experiences tend to discourage the use of drama in the church and to dampen one's enthusiasm for writing plays, whether to be read or to be acted. However, drama, through liturgy and morality plays, has long played an effective part in the teaching life of the Christian Church. It may be that once the idea of the value of drama is accepted, hidden talent will be revealed.

For example, in seeking to present the Maundy Thursday experience vividly to my congregation I wrote and presented the following morality play. It is true that inspiration for this play was sought over a long period of time, and the idea was nurtured continuously for days before the words were ready to be written on paper. It may be that such a thought will never occur to you, or if it does it may never get into usable form. Nevertheless, we should make the attempt to discover for ourselves if some dormant talent in this field cannot be aroused and utilized for the spread of His kingdom.

The technique will vary, but usually first will come the desire, then the imagination's search for the setting and the theme, and at last the jotting down of ideas, characters, and

Scripture to be used. The actual writing will be either the slowly-pieced-together or manufactured way, or the inspired all-down-at-one-sitting way, depending on how each one's mind works. A bit of experimenting should do the trick. Charles Rann Kennedy's *The Terrible Meek* furnished the impetus and the pattern for *In the Night*. The need for a new presentation of the Maundy Thursday theme gave the point and purpose of it.

In the Night
A One-Act Morality Play

Persons of the play: Peter, James, and John. Time: The darkest moment just before dawn on Good Friday. Place: An upper room. Setting: At the top of the chancel steps a table and three stools. A candle or oil lamp on table. No other properties. Costumes: Loosely fitting black robes or cassocks.

The preparation: Minister stands in opening to sanctuary, and explains in this fashion: The church from ancient times has given miracle plays during the holy seasons, with the purpose of preparing hearts and minds for Holy Communion and for Easter Day. This is to make vivid the essential meaning of this night, to show why we have this service of remembrance. Let all be silent with an attitude of quiet remembering.

Music diminishes as all lights are extinguished. Lights nearest cross on altar last to go out. Then darkness. Choir then sings a hymn or appropriate music. The organ music continues quietly, slowly fading to a mere background of sound. Out of silent dark comes a voice.

THE PROLOGUE: " In the night he was betrayed he gave thanks . . ." and afterward departed for a hillside near at

hand, with his friends by his side. The darkness was fresh
and cool, filled with the thousand unseen voices of the night.
Peace was there and close comradeship. Not even the
shadows spoke of the near moments to come. Danger was
far away — or was it that his presence made all living things
deaf to fear? The friends were weary from trying to remember, and fearful of forgetting too soon, precious words
beyond their complete understanding. " In the night " he
was betrayed he uttered them and gave thanks for memories
to print them on, even though time must pass ere their
focussed meaning would be projected beyond an upper
room and an olive garden. Sleep came and dreams. He
prayed.

But sleep and prayer and the noises of the night were
shivered into cold reality by tramping feet. . . . They took
him, the betrayed, and led him away in the night. . . . And
his heart gave thanks that the seed had found a garden rich
and firm in which to grow and be protected.

Back into silence the hillside slipped, deep silence as if
death had possessed the darkness and stilled it forever . . .
no friends, no murmur of bugs and wind moths, no enemies
. . . nothing but the soft mantle of nothingness.

(Music swells here then continues quietly.)

Shortly after midnight, along the moon-swept streets, two
figures, James and John, crept silently, save for a pebble's
turning, and stealthily, up the outer stairs into an upper
room, a room still warm with body warmth and the lingering
scent of wine and broken bread, there to hide until the
danger was well past. They drew close together in the
center of the room. After a moment of frantic breathing
they dared light a wisp of light. (The flame is lighted.)
They whispered puzzling questions back and forth. Listen.
. . . (The music stops. The flame flickers until the two
are calm.)

THE PLAY: (James is seated at center of table — John down right.)

James: For very fear I could not remain — it drove me away from him.

John: How could this thing have happened? Our fear and his capture?

James: Yes, how could it have happened to him? We never feared for him — only for our following. Even as we boasted, we trembled at the thought of following to the end.

John: Only one was missing after we left this room. No one else knew where we would be.

James: It was Judas. He it was who spoiled it all. I saw him at the head of the soldiers. He it was who must have led them to the garden.

John: How could Judas have betrayed him? Judas loved him, too.

James: He must have been out of his mind.

John: Yes, out of mind and bereft of heart.

(A brief moment of quiet. James rises.)

James: Why did the end of our great mission, our great dream have to be like this? If we had only stayed awake to protect him. But we could not even watch one hour.

John: He did not want violence. He rebuked Peter's rashness in attacking one of the soldiers. No, we could have done nothing. The fellowship is broken in sunder. He will soon be dead, I know it . . . (chokes sobbingly).

James: " Dead " — that is no word for him! He will never be dead to us. He will live in our hearts even though to remember breaks them.

John: Failure has come at the road's end — at the end of the endless road stretching but yesterday as far as the eye could see, and beyond — a ribbon of bright glory leading to the kingdom.

James: Kingdom no more — but a few dying embers of a

grand and noble scheme, flung back now into the past whence it came — a dream future and a buried past — never a present reality.

(A long silence — movement by the two — signs of prayer on their lips. A cock crows in the distance. Suddenly a hurried step and with a rush Peter enters down left with hair and clothes awry. James and John start up — the candle flame stirs violently.)

James: It is Peter. (Relief is in his voice.)

Peter: Did you hear it? It crowed again. He said it would. I have denied him thrice in the courtyard, and I swore I would not. It was I who bragged I'd go with him even unto death. What made me deny him and myself? It was stupid fear. That clumsy wielding of the sword was but panic and no more. I left my faith and my courage behind in the garden as I fled away from him. Oh, my God. (He drops to a seat at the table. James puts hand on Peter's shoulder.)

John: We all deserted him, Peter. We were no match for them.

James: Just a few short hours have passed and our joy has spent itself, and sorrow weaves our moments as it were a shroud.

Peter: I told him I'd die for him — I promised him — God forgive me. (Pause. Then Peter jumps up.) But I *am* willing to die for him, to die in his stead if need be, even though I have deserted and denied. He will forgive me and give me another chance, I know. (He mumbles to himself.) " Seventy times seven."

John: The Master said many words as we ate together — words that are beginning to burn their truth into my mind. Peter, remember the outcry you made over the feet-washing ceremony?

Peter: How well do I remember.

John: Remember how he rebuked us by this deed as we argued loudly over who should be the first?

James: I tremble with amazement as I think back on it — the loving humility of it.

John: I was *ashamed* and all thoughts and feelings of my position of privilege in being close to the Master left me.

James: He bade us love each other so much we would be always humble and thoughtful one of the other.

Peter: Did he not say, " You are not all of you clean " ?

James: Yes, and the meaning comes to the point of sense. No, not *all* clean — there is still fear to be washed away.

Peter: And denial. . . .

John: And desertion.

Peter: What else did he say? I do not remember so easily; my hands are bigger than my mind.

John: Many things — so many things — let me recall some of them. (Pause.) He said we must believe in him just as we believe in God. He told Thomas that by knowing him we also knew God. He told us a lot about going away — about preparing a place for us, about not leaving us friendless. . . .

James: Yes, and he said the world would not see him but we would, because he would still live on with us. . . .

Peter: But I do not understand. It is all so bewildering, my mind aches with desire and is held back.

John: His words — he spoke them for us to remember in the darkness. Remember, he spoke of the vine and oneness with the Father and of us as the branches?

James: Yes, I remember, especially how he said we would be persecuted if we followed him. Our fear has prevented these promised wonders. (With new courage) We must believe in him; we must have faith in him as *The Way*, and we *must* follow, come what may.

Peter: I am ready. Forgiveness has released my fear. I do not understand but I believe. I shall not falter again. This much I know, not by possessing it with my slippery mind, but by a strong anchoring certainty in my heart which my mind will obey.

John: He said, " I am leaving the world but I shall come again and no matter what trouble may come, be thankful and take courage for I have made it possible for you to conquer all such worldliness."

James: And he prayed a prayer, like forged links of gold in a golden chain — upward and upward to God the Father. There was oneness there, and God bound us as one while he prayed.

John: The dawn will discover us and reveal us too soon. There is work to do. Memory, with its tireless feet, is eager to wend its way through me; there is an urging within me.

James: We must tell the others and gather them together; we must be ready to witness and to brandish his words as a fiery sword.

John: We must ever remember this night and the new life it has brought to the dying called fear. We must keep near for use this tiny flame and the words which made its light a steady burning. In the night . . . he gave thanks, for he was the dawn of our understanding soon to break.

Peter: Aye, full meaning soon to break, that love is the only power; that because of it our chains are cut away and we are free; that Christ came not to make our way easier but to make men great. Quickly, while there is yet time. We are armed with our faith and prepared to face the days of battle to be won. We came with fear — but fearless we go. . . . (Music begins again quietly but urgently as James extinguishes the light.)

THE EPILOGUE: (The Voice speaks again.) One by one the three, restored and with single mind, left the room and darted down the crooked streets, eager to proclaim the open way. They went unnoticed ere the sun took over the day and shone down upon its shame. No return to the old tasks now, strangely unalluring, or to the old life, as they had thought, disillusioned, to face the mocking voices of those who had never caught and followed the vision — the vision where all would be God's kind of kingdom and power and glory, the kind built upon his love, the kind which would endure forever.

They had a promise given in memory stored. They had a way and a truth and on this first Good Friday they had a life — a life which sustained them to journey's end, and kept them to their following.

(Choir sings an appropriate anthem in the darkness, such as "Bread of the World." Candles on altar relighted during last part of anthem. Lights come up gradually, beginning nearest cross — never in nave, if Holy Communion is to follow. Minister is at altar to begin celebration of the Holy Communion as lights are up and music is ended.)

*   *   *

Now for a slightly different form of dramatic presentation. In order to get across a difficult point at the very special Christmas season, a miniature drama of redemption was written and read to a congregation at an afternoon service. (Incidentally, Lloyd C. Douglas won his way to an almost world-wide pulpit by such a technique at his Sunday-evening service.)

Lonely Soul
A Miniature Drama of Redemption

Characters: An expectant mother with an illegitimate child, soon to be born — representing any woman in distress resulting from sin. God — a voice within.

Setting: A bare room on Christmas Eve (or any other day of sharpened contrast) which is meagerly furnished.

Curtain rises on figure of woman sitting huddled in a chair. She is obviously miserable. Her face is drawn from much spiritual conflict and suffering. We hear voices but her lips do not move.

Woman: I am all alone, forgotten. No one cares. . . .

Voice: But I am here with you.

Woman: Who are you?

Voice: I am the still small voice you've only now begun to hear.

Woman: Oh, no, I've listened and listened and you never spoke.

Voice: I spoke but your fears made it impossible for you to hear. I've been calling you for a long time.

Woman: But why didn't you speak more loudly and force me to hear, when you knew how desperately I needed you?

Voice: I could not have done that, for then you would have had no choice, and so you would have rebelled against me, and your obedience to my commands would have been unwilling and joyless.

Woman: Now that I do hear, please leave me not; speak words of comfort, cure my loneliness, ease my pain. . . .

Voice: Wait, is there not first another job to be done? Must there not first be a covenant between us, so that we know exactly where we stand?

Woman: As you will, but hurry, or else I'll go out of my mind.

Voice: You have not yet sought me, as I have long sought you. You have not yet asked of me. No word or action from you has yet revealed a single desire beyond selfishness — to be rid of your suffering. You alone can never be victorious over it.

Woman: I do now turn and ask forgiveness for my faithless fears and worldly anxieties — will this bring release?

Voice: Yes, re-lease, a new lease on life, comes as you really

lazily into the mouthpiece. " Yes, this is the sheriff's office."
As the excited voice at the other end of the line spoke with
a shrill nasal tone in an uninterrupted flow, Deputy Glum
perked up. His eyes opened fully, he dropped the cigarette
drooping at the corner of his mouth, he straightened up from
his slouch and spoke with energy before he slammed down
the receiver, " We'll be right out."

" Sheriff, oh, Sheriff Dither, someone just called and said
they'd found a dead man nailed to an old tree stump at the
edge of old man Harum's burned-over clearing. No, they
found nothing and left the body there. They think it is the
leader of a crazy group of religious fanatics in Bell Hollow."

Sheriff Dither and Deputy Glum rushed out from the
fly-specked cubbyhole adjoining the jail, jumped into the
city's best department car, a dilapidated Model T Ford, and
headed toward old Harum's place, the scene of the killing.

" Never heard of anything like it 'round these parts,
Sheriff. We've had shootin's and hangin's and knifin's and
drownin's but no nailin's. Wonder who did it and why? "

" Save your wonderin', Glum, till we see what's what."

By the time they arrived quite a crowd had gathered and
were gazing curiously and wonderingly at the dead man on
the barren tree. The sheriff looked at the body hanging
limply, held up mainly by a stout rope under his armpits.
But the nails through the center of each outstretched hand
were tenpenny at least. There was little blood, save in the
side, approximately where the appendix was. A red stain
showed on the man's shirt. Probably a knife wound, the
sheriff thought. The man on the tree was about forty, of
medium height, with chestnut hair. His face was fair and
even in death was lifelike. No fear or worry lined his face.
He had died at peace within. His clothes were coarse and
worn.

" Get a ladder, Glum, and several men. Take the body

down. Cy Young's hearse'll be here soon." The sheriff gave
directions as he sized up the situation. "Get over to that
clearing, all of you," he bellowed to the little crowd. "I
want to know what's been going on out here."

They moved slowly, even reluctantly, away from the
awesome scene. There was a fascination about a man who
died in such a manner which held them. They did not want
to leave. But leave they must.

"Now what do you know? Speak up, each one of you.
The sooner you speak the quicker you can go."

The first one to dare utterance was a short, stocky farmer,
Sniper by name, who had the adjoining property to Harum's.

"Sheriff, we all know him. He's been here about a year,
working around the farms occasionally, living awhile at one
place, then another. But he spent most of his time preachin'
and talkin'. He wasn't a regular preacher, mind you, just
kind of picked it up, I gather. A lot of folks liked him and,
so far as I know, he did no harm. But a few of the people
grew dissatisfied with their own churches and preachers and
formed a little group around him. They called themselves
'Followers.' Don't know what they did or believed, but the
ministers and some of the church members were pretty sore
at him for comin' in and breakin' up their flocks."

"He's right, Sheriff," said Mrs. Pepper. "They were all
envious of him. He was a most interesting man. He never
shouted when he preached and he was so nice to people. I
had a mind to go his way myself."

The sheriff broke in. "Do you mean to tell me somebody
killed him because he preached and won a few converts
from the other churches?"

"Of course not, Sheriff. It is true he preached a somewhat
different doctrine from us, but we didn't hate him or wish
him harm." Brother Sparkless defended the cloth.

"Strange goin's on," the sheriff said, "but we'll find out
who did it and why."

The body was taken down and the tree was bare, save for the rope still hanging from one branch. The hearse took the body away as the sheriff got a " lead " from a young man from over the creek, who was a " follower." As the hearse rattled off the young man spoke:

" They killed him, Sheriff, for he made them all feel guilty and ashamed. They were jealous and envious and could not stand seeing him around. They killed him, I swear it. And he never harmed nobody."

After the young " follower " made his accusation that " they " had killed the man on a tree, the crowd was in an uproar. Denials were on every mouth. They threatened to do him violence. Deputy Glum stepped in and protected him. When Sheriff Dither could be heard above the tumult, he said to the crowd, " There's been enough violence for one day in this place. Now keep quiet till we're done." Then to the young " follower " who was standing silent now with bowed head. " Who are 'they,' Son? Who did you mean when you said ' they killed him ' ? "

The young man hesitated, then slowly replied: " It was all of them who hated him. They started false rumors about him and made people misunderstand his words and his work. That is why he was killed."

" But who tied him up and drove the nails, and stabbed him in the side? " The sheriff put the question impatiently.

" That I do not know. But may God forgive them all." The young man attempted to walk away.

" Just a minute there," called out Deputy Glum, " no one leaves until we know a lot more about these goin's on."

"Anyone else want to speak? " the sheriff asked.

" It may not help much, but I know two men who were seen in the vicinity early this morning, scurrying away from here in a hurry; my husband recognized them both." Miranda Buzzyer spoke with authority.

"Well, who were they? Speak up." The sheriff wanted clues, evidence, the guilty parties.

The crowd listened eagerly for the names. Miranda was fully aware of her importance and prolonged the scene as long as possible. " Silas, that's my husband, Sheriff, said he thought it was funny Simon Simple was hereabouts. He hadn't seen him for quite a spell. Simon once hired out to us, but he got so no 'count we let him go. The other one he thought was Beal Turner, a bootlegger from Arls Gap, but he wasn't sure. It was early morning and the light was still dim. Better see Silas, Sheriff."

" Sheriff, I'll go fetch Silas Buzzyer," spoke Deputy Glum.

"No, wait a minute. We'll see him later. Get the names of every one here. We may want to see them again. After that, go call the office. Tell Sergeant Domb to send out an alarm on Simon Simple and Beal Turner. We have a description of Beal in the rogue's gallery. See old Harum for one of Simon. Get along fast."

The sheriff looked over the dozen or so people clustered in front of him in the partial shade of a fire-scarred pine. " Does anyone know anything else? " A long silence. The sheriff looked from face to face. As his eyes sought each one they turned away and would not look him in the eye. That is, all but one, a comely young woman of thirty or so, light of hair, and not so roughly clad as the rest. She met his gaze steadfastly. The sheriff did not know her, but liked her looks. He thought: "How did this beauty get here? " He said, " Where do you fit in? You're not a farmer's wife. You're a stranger, aren't you? "

" Yes, I'm the new schoolteacher. My name is Susan Prey and I knew the man who died on that tree. I came when the word spread. I left the school in charge of another. May I speak a good word for Brother John? "

"Any word, Miss Prey, any word that will shed light on this case, any word at all, good or bad."

" He helped me. Not in any one instance, but it helped me just to hear him and see his face. He had such a strong face and I believe he loved everyone. He lived the religion he professed. It was a simple gospel he preached, Sheriff, mostly one of love and the removal of everything which prevented our loving. He was as spirit-filled and as godly a man as I ever knew. I shall never forget his favorite admonition to us as we departed from a meeting together. When he spoke it sounded like a prayer — ' Remember Jesus Christ.' Why could anyone hate him or spread false rumors about him or kill him? "

Her eyes filled with tears and her voice choked, and she could say no more.

" I have all the names, Sheriff," the deputy reported.

" Everyone may go now, but we'll want to talk with some of you later. Keep within easy reach. Glum, go get Silas and meet me at Query's store in half an hour."

The sheriff's head throbbed as he sauntered over to the general store to piece together what he'd heard and to wait for reports from the office and for Glum and Silas. " No word against Brother John yet," he thought, " not a single word."

" Now, Silas, tell me about Simon Simple and Beal Turner, and what connection you think they might have with this murder."

Silas Buzzyer, Deputy Glum, and Sheriff Dither were seated in the general store, with store-owner Query within earshot in the background, and a curious group still hanging around outside.

" Well, Sheriff, I know Simon all right. He's a bit queer in the head; was always hearin' things that weren't. But I never knew him to hurt anything. Wait a minute, I do recall one thing. It was an old dog we had that an auto had struck.

Simon couldn't bear to see it suffer and he killed it. Poor dog couldn't have lived, anyway."

"Are you sure it was Simon you saw this morning? "

"Oh, it was Simon all right, and he was moving quickly toward the dense woods, away from where that man was nailed up. He was with another fellow, Beal Turner, I'm most positive."

The sheriff kept pushing Silas. " But could you swear it? He is a notorious character, you know."

" I wouldn't swear it, but I'm pretty sure. Beal and I were good friends when we was growin' up. But the idea of easy money went to his head. Honest farmin' wasn't good enough. ' Work too hard and get too little,' he said to me. Ran a still over in Bell Hollow until the preachers got down on him."

" The preachers got down on him, you say? " asked Sheriff Dither.

" Yes, even threatened to tar and feather him for manufacturin' so much demon rum. Say, maybe. . . ."

" Maybe what? " the sheriff caught quickly at a possible clue.

" Nothing, I guess, just thought he might have killed the man to please the preachers, and paid Simon to help him carry the body to the clearing after he'd stabbed him to death."

" Now isn't that a pretty theory." The sheriff was sarcastic. Silas was treading on his preserves. But in a moment his face changed. A light dawned. " But that knife wound — you may be right. Just a minute."

The sheriff hurried to the telephone and called the jail. Someone answered. The sheriff spoke.

" What have they found out about the cause of death? "

The information poured into the sheriff's ears.

" Thanks. Anything on Simple and Turner yet? O.K., keep in touch."

The light on the sheriff's face had gone out. He turned slowly and came back to his seat and sat down heavily.

"That's funny. The Doc says the knife wound was not serious enough to cause death, nor were the lacerations in his hands. And he wasn't left up long enough for exposure to do it. They have found no adequate cause for his death."

Deputy Glum had been listening until now. But words came as the sheriff paused to puzzle over the latest news.

"I remember some of the things the people said, as I stood among them when we first came. One lady, a 'follower' of his, I think, said, 'He is not dead, I know.' Another woman said, 'They broke his heart.' A man said, and he was a 'follower,' 'He told us this would happen. That men would kill and think they did the Lord's bidding.' An old codger with a scraggly white beard said, 'Some say the feller was a Jew. Dunno, though; can't say from his looks.' There were a lot of things the people said, but one thing I heard several times, from his 'followers' and those who hardly knew him at all. It was a strange phrase to hear at a killin'. I remember it exactly. 'The Hollow's been different since he came.' They didn't say what was different about it, though."

"That's enough, Glum; right now we must concentrate on more evidence for pinning the murder on someone. Let's go back to town." Then to Silas: "We may need you to identify these two when we pick them up." The sheriff got up and moved toward the door, with Glum at his heels. "Keep by the phone, Query; may want to call one of these witnesses."

While the sheriff was on his way back to his stuffy, smelly tobacco-juice-stained office, a small meeting was being held deep in the woods. Inside a small square frame building, built alongside Bitter Water Creek, completely buried in the trees, a group of the "followers" were meeting. The leader was a tall husky farmer of middle years; Temple was his name. He was speaking solemnly to the half-dozen or so persons present.

". . . and so we must not worry about Brother John. Nor must we be concerned about those who killed him. We must feel deep sorrow for them and pray for them. We shall bury him tomorrow from this place, under the shade of the white dogwood clump yonder by Bitter Water Creek. We must not mourn but rejoice. Now we can really discover our strength and our faith."

In the silence after this speech they all remembered Brother John and felt him there with them.

But in the sheriff's office, upon his return, was a shocking bit of news. Beal Turner had been captured, but Simon Simple, so Beal said, had been hit by a truck and killed, and Beal had buried him.

Beal Turner was sullen. He refused to talk after his initial statement about Simon's death. Sheriff Dither questioned him for hours. Now he was ready to give Beal up for the time being. But before he could give the order for Deputy Glum to take him away, Beal changed his mind and spoke.

"I might as well tell you, Sheriff; you'll find out sooner or later anyway. I'll tell you the truth as I know it."

Sheriff Dither tilted back in his squeaky, rattly swivel chair, which had more tilt to it than swivel, the strain of uncertainty clearing a little from his face. Deputy Glum leaned against the corner of the rolltop desk, as usual slouching in a tired pose, with a cigarette hanging from that certain spot in the corner of his mouth. Beal sat to one side in a battered kitchen chair, with an air of eagerness and relief at the decision he'd made. He spoke deliberately though, at first weighing each word carefully. He never forgot he was a lawbreaker talking to a sheriff. This made him cagey.

"Simon was the helper in my business."

The sheriff grunted audibly at the words "my business" and almost smiled.

"He knew everyone, and everyone knew him. He got around and kept me posted on customers and possible disturbances to my business. He told me what the local preachers thought. But that didn't worry me. It never hurt my business. That is, until the big co-operative revival last fall when I was held up as the devil in disguise. Then my business really was hurt. I hated these pious, meddlin' parsons. But I couldn't do anything except stay out of their reach. Then one day Simon told me they'd found another scapegoat, this new preacher, Brother John. They had it in for him because he got converts in a quiet way and won some of the best members of their churches, although they didn't leave their churches, but just attended Brother John's meetings too. Simon said he heard also they were against him for being different — his group of followers had no name and no official standing; for being a pacifist — he believed in the power of nonviolence; for talking against the poll tax, because it meant discrimination against the poor; and there were other things. I don't remember them all. I figured we were in the same boat. We were both in bad odor with the churchgoing crowd. So I planned to see him and work out a deal. The other night Simon led me to the meeting place down on Bitter Water Creek. We waited until the prayer service was over, then I accosted Brother John and walked with him toward his abiding place with Farmer Temple. I told him how I felt. That we ought to stick together. But he just smiled at me and said, 'Fear not what men say.' I couldn't make him see it my way. He always had an answer to everything. I can't remember all he said, but I concluded nothing bothered him except men's disobedience to God's laws. This made me mad. 'Just another pious preacher who thinks he's better than me,' I thought. My tongue lashed him but I made no impression. His very calm infuriated me. I couldn't bear the sight of him nor the sound of his words."

Beal's words tumbled out and he was greatly agitated. "Something rebelled in me and choked me and blinded me. I wanted to get rid of him. He made me dissatisfied with my plan and my work. In fury I whipped out my knife and let him have it in the side. It was automatic. I didn't know what I was doing. He fell without a word. I thought I'd killed him and started to run, but Simon, whom I had forgotten, stopped me. 'Mr. Turner,' he said, without a trace of feeling, 'you've killed him and he was such a good man. We must nail him to a tree, a tree shaped like a cross. All good men like him die on crosses.' It sounded crazy, but I was in a frenzy, and since Simon knew all that had happened, I wanted to please him. So I helped him carry Brother John to the clearing, and Simon, with a rope and nails and hammer he got from somewhere, tied him up, then nailed his hands carefully to a charred stump of a tree with two stout limbs outstretched, and we left him there for dead. I took Simon with me. But he kept saying, 'Brother John was such a good man and all men like him die on crosses.' Simon said once, as we ran along in the night, 'But he's not really dead, just dead for three days.' I didn't know what he meant, but I did feel all sore and shaken within. I couldn't forget the man. But my remorse was not the worst of it. It was the remembrance of his eyes as he looked at me when I struck him. You know the rest, Sheriff. God, I'm glad that's over." He had slumped back into his sullen mood.

The sheriff sat glued to his chair. Deputy Glum had forgotten to draw on his cigarette. There was silence save for a dozen flies zooming after each other in the heavy air toward the ceiling.

Sheriff Dither had the murderer, but the coroner had said neither the knife nor the nails had caused his death. But the sheriff kept these thoughts to himself. He finally gathered the energy to swing back his springless chair to upright, got up and said to Deputy Glum:

"Take him back and lock him up; we've got some more work to do."

The schoolteacher and the fair young man who had borne witness that day when it happened, both of them faithful "followers," were chosen to prepare the meeting place for the service to be held before Brother John's burial in the midst of the dogwood clump by the side of Bitter Water Creek. They had lovingly bedecked the little plain square wooden building with flowers and branches of flowering shrub. The place was alive with the beautiful sights and odors of life, "of life never ending," as Brother John put it. The job was finished. They came out into the night air, still and cool. The moon was full and coated the meeting-house with a silver sheen. It lay upon the trees and made a bright pattern on the ground beneath, as it filtered through the first budding leaves.

The schoolteacher spoke. "It was a night like this long ago, when the time for the Easter festival came. The season of the full spring moon, a variable festival following the appearance of the moon in its splendor, was chosen so that the pilgrims could have light by night along the often dangerous roads. This night is almost too beautiful."

They walked slowly toward the sound of the creek, which they could see sparkling as its ripples caught the light from a bright moonbeam.

"It is full springtime again," the young man said. "Nature

is being reborn, but man is yet to be reborn. God is moving in the earth tonight and I feel he is about to manifest his power and glory again. The life flowing all around seems to be swelling up to choke out death. Brother John said ' death is helpless before the power of God, even though it is grim and determined in its resistance.' What about Brother John? Why did he have to be taken after so short a stay with us? What shall we do for a leader? I am still so uncertain and weak."

" I've thought about that question, too," the schoolteacher replied, " and can find but few answers. Brother John died, I think, from the shock of realizing sinful man could still be so perverse and unseeing, even after Jesus had died to make man see. His great sorrow was this — that man with the glorious life of the spirit at hand, with every power and happiness at his disposal, could still choose darkness and evil, still choose to keep his life narrow and unfulfilled. He was bewildered to learn that man could slam the door to freedom, and through his pettiness, his twisted attitudes, his thoughtlessness, his continual disobedience to the obvious laws of God, choke out goodness. Brother John was so sensitive to the needs of others that their sinfulness broke his heart, long before he died."

" But how could he let all this affect him so, when he knew the love and power of God to change men were available and had been used by him to win our few faithful ones to a new life? " The young man was frankly puzzled and concerned. They stopped in the clearing in the center of the dogwood grove where they were to bury Brother John on the morrow. Even in the soft moonlight, the brown stain on the white dogwood blooms, symbolical of the nail prints in the Master's hands, could be plainly seen. But the tinge of red in the center of the blossoms did not show.

" I guess the burden of the accumulated deceit, hatred,

resentment, impurity, nastiness, greed, consuming selfishness, disregard for human decency, waste of life and misuse
of God's gift, became a cross which he carried and at last
erected for himself. He died, I think, for the redemption
of all those around here who refused to see or to hear, to
open up or to accept the Master's way, which he had discovered led to life's fullness and life's true meaning."

"They say Simon Simple nailed him to that tree and that
Beal Turner knifed him." The young man was thinking
aloud. "Simon was a kindly man, like a child. He did it
for some strange kind of love and belief about the cross.
Beal was a sinful man and found the result of his sinning
to be another's death and perhaps his own."

"That is not ours to know," the schoolteacher added.
"We must forgive them because of him."

The little meeting place was crowded with the faithful
few and the curious many. All the good church folk came
out of a sense of duty, or perhaps of guilt. Many more were
outside listening at the open windows. Even the sheriff and
Deputy Glum were present. Farmer Temple conducted the
brief, beautiful service. His words rang out with no sad
note in them and became Brother John's last message to his
friends and neighbors and "those" who killed him. The
beauty of nature's abundance around the square meetinghouse and overhead was in strange and weird contrast with
the burned-over section near at hand which nature had not
yet redeemed. In one was the memory of a death. In the
other a profuse reminder of life. Farmer Temple began with
the final lines from Wordsworth's famous "Ode" and continued with Brother John's favorite passages from 1 John
(5:1-4) and 1 Peter (1:3-5). The only other sound than
his strong deep voice was a bird calling, a bee buzzing, and
the faint ripple of the quick-flowing creek.

"And O ye Fountains, Meadows, Hills, and Groves,
Forebode not any severing of our loves! Yet in my heart
of hearts I feel your might;
I only have relinquished one delight, to live beneath your
more habitual sway."

No one stirred save to moisten dry lips.

". . . Another race hath been, and other palms are won.
Thanks to the human heart by which we live,
Thanks to its tenderness, its joys, and fears,
To me the meanest flower that blows can give
Thoughts that do often lie too deep for tears."

" Everyone who believes that Jesus is the Christ is a child
of God, and everyone who loves the Father loves those who
are his children. This is how we can be sure that we love
the children of God: it is by loving God and obeying his
commands. For loving God means obeying his commands,
and his commands are not burdensome, for every child of
God is victorious over the world. Our faith is the victory
that has triumphed over the world. . . .
" Blessed be the God and Father of our Lord Jesus Christ!
In his great mercy he has caused us to be born anew to a life
of hope through Jesus Christ's resurrection from the dead,
and to an imperishable, unsullied, and unfading inheritance
. . . and you by God's power are being protected through
faith to receive a salvation that is now ready to be disclosed. . . ." [1]
Farmer Temple finished speaking. Not a sound. Not a
movement. But within each heart and mind thunderbirds
of the spirit were beating their wings.

[1] From *The Bible, An American Translation.* Smith and Goodspeed.
Used by permission of the University of Chicago Press.

The trial was over. Beal Turner got ten years in the penitentiary for the murder of Brother John. He said he was glad of a chance to pay for his part in the crime. He had taken his full share of the blame, too, during the trial. He could have pinned it all on Simon Simple, who was dead anyway, but he acted as though he wanted to be found guilty, as though he wanted to make up for as much as he could. It was a peculiar trial. Beal was never proved to be the actual murderer but his record of bootlegging went against him. Over night, Brother John had become famous and people were asking about him and his sect of Christians. It had sobered and bettered the people who lived in the Hollow and round about. He seemed to be a stronger influence dead than he had ever been alive.

The sheriff tried to forget the whole thing, but it came back to him, almost haunted him. One day, three weeks after the trial, he drove down past Query's store, to Bitter Water Creek just above the meetinghouse. No one was about. He got out of the creaking old Model T Ford, which had wheezed to a stall, with a jet of steam spurting with a hiss from the dull brass radiator cap. He sat down under a tree at the water's edge. He took off his hat and laid it carelessly aside. He leaned back against a weeping willow tree trunk and made himself comfortable. His eyes shifted from the clear water running past in a hurry at his feet to the weatherbeaten meetinghouse ugly in the sunlight, to the clump of dogwood still blooming, to the charred clearing. Yes, he could just make out the stump, too. His thoughts gathered up the incidents of the past few weeks. He tried to see them objectively, as a whole, with perspective. He went back over the discovery of Brother John's body nailed to the dead tree stump with a knife wound in his side; the persons involved — Simon Simple and Beal Turner — seen in the vicinity of the crime; the jealous preachers who didn't like the competition; the leading disciples of Brother John — the beautiful schoolteacher, the fair young man, the strong husky Farmer Temple. He thought of the questions and answers leading to Beal's confession, the coroner's report of death from other causes than knife and nail wounds, the talk which had gone around of his dying of shock or a broken heart. He went back over the trial. It had produced nothing much save a unanimous feeling of regret over Brother John's death and the actual joy of Beal over his judgment. The sheriff heard that Farmer Temple had spent several hours with him before the trial. He remembered Brother John's funeral and how the little wooden meetinghouse was transformed. If that was what Brother John preached and lived and taught, then he couldn't have been so much of a threat to the other churches, except to make them check the power and reality of their own professed religion. The sheriff still could not understand it. He noticed that Deputy Glum had been attending meetings of Brother John's "followers" whenever he could. Farmer Temple had taken temporary charge. Sheriff Dither wanted to go himself, but he couldn't. He belonged to another church and was afraid they wouldn't understand.

Many consciences were cutting deep into the daily life of Bell Hollow. There seemed to be a new spirit at work. The sheriff had felt it and seen it. He had actually seen one of the local ministers stop Farmer Temple on the street and express his sorrow over their loss, and wish him "Godspeed." The more the sheriff thought, the less he could figure things out. As he continued his reverie in the cool shady spot on the creek bank, one thought haunted him: "Am I to blame in any way?" This same question was being asked in a hundred hearts or more.

A crack of a twig and the thud of a foot jerked him erect.

"Oh, it's you, Farmer Temple. I thought — never mind. Sit down, won't you?"

" No, Sheriff, I can't. I'm on my way to the schoolhouse to tell the news which just came. She must know. We'll all meet late in the afternoon. Won't you come? "

" What's up? " The sheriff got quickly to his feet.

" It doesn't sound possible, but word has come that Brother John is preaching in place after place over the ridge." Farmer Temple's face shone with excitement and credulous wonder.

The sheriff didn't know what to say and when the words came they seemed not his own. " That is what happened to the Nazarene. This whole business is like — Temple, you don't think — surely — it couldn't be."

" It might be, Sheriff, we shall see. Won't you come and meet with us? "

" I'll be there," the sheriff murmured quietly, yet with a sudden flash of insight and confidence. Farmer Temple took great strides across the creek, down the path leading to the one-room schoolhouse, and was soon gone out of sight.

The sheriff stood there bareheaded. He raised his eyes and looked through the twirling green leaves dancing to the hurdy-gurdy tune of a fitful breeze. No one was there to hear. But the words which fell from his lips were, " It might have been —" as he started toward Brother John's grave.

CHAPTER VIII

THE MESSAGE IN PAGEANTS

In divers manners spake.
HEBREWS 1:1

S TILL ANOTHER form of dramatic material is the pageant. The illustration gives, I hope, more than the usual narrow concept to the great missionary command of winning the whole world for Christ. " Thy Kingdom Come " was presented in the Municipal Auditorium, Beaumont, Texas.

Thy Kingdom Come

A Pageant Presenting the Missionary Work of the Church

PROLOGUE. Vision — " He is not dead, He is risen! "

Scene 1 — The Hudson Stuck Memorial Hospital. Alaska. Medicine
Scene 2 — St. Paul's Vestry. Not sold
Scene 3 — Emery Hall School for Girls. Liberia. Alone
Scene 4 — The Every Member Canvass. Refusal
Scene 5 — China. Plight
Scene 6 — Woman's Guild. Blind
Scene 7 — The Bishop's Office. Diocesan Missions

INTERLUDE. Work — " The fields are white unto the harvest."

Scene 8 — Old Barnlett. " Scrooge of Christ "

EPILOGUE. Inspiration — " Thy Kingdom Come "

Setting: Three-tiered elevation with broad steps and wide platform at top, for background. Two columns rising at either end, with mock rood beam connecting. A lighted cross in top center of beam. Setting draped in white or cream. Blue cyclorama for the entire background.

Chorus: To be arranged in two parts. One group behind cyclorama center, to be vested, and framed in between columns and rood beam in tiers at the climax. The other group in balcony or backstage. The organ will be off stage right, or at most convenient point for directing chorus and seeing players.

Lighting: Use no borders, foots, or floods. Only spots — as indicated in scenes.

PROLOGUE

(Stage dark, except for lighted cross center stage, as curtain parts. Very quiet organ music is heard. Perhaps the whisper of a hymn sung by the chorus. Out of this music, and coming from the center of the cross, the Voice is heard.)

Voice: Jesus Christ, the same yesterday, today, and forever.

(The organ swells into opening chorus, with stage still darkened.)

Voice: Jesus was dead. His disciples were discouraged. All hope was gone. Their dreams had been shattered. Nothing remained except sorrowful memories. Back to humdrum daily tasks. The Messiah was still to come. Suddenly, like a flash of lightning from the sky, came the thrilling message. (Light in cross grows brighter.)

(As music dies away, spotlight reveals dimly group in center stage beneath the cross, in characteristic poses. Pin spot picks out character who is speaking. Strive for group effect with no action. Use colored spots. Organ continues to weave a delicate background of music throughout Prologue, following and marking each changing mood.)

Voices: (Different ones repeating over and over) He is not dead, He is risen!

Voice: Yes, He was alive, for He was seen of Mary in the garden at dawn.

Mary: Master!

Voice: He was also seen in an upper room in Emmaus by two disciples.

Cleopas: It is the Master. He is not dead but alive.

Other Disciple: We must hasten to Jerusalem to tell the good news.

Voice: He appeared unto the eleven twice. Once in the presence of Thomas the Doubter.

Thomas: Lord, I believe.

Voice: The news spread that Jesus was alive. Many witnesses saw him. For forty days he was seen of men. Then came his ascension. These words he left behind for his Disciples — the Missionary Command of Our Lord.

Voice of Jesus: Go therefore and make disciples of all nations, baptizing them in the name of the Father and of the Son and of the Holy Ghost; teaching them to observe all things whatsoever I commanded you: and lo, I am with you always, even unto the end of the world.

Voice: The revelation had come. The final injunction had been given and received. The disciples' spirits were revived. They took fresh courage. They began to remember and to tell His words, His actions, the story of His life and ministry. They left behind once again their daily tasks to follow Him. They told the " Good News " everywhere, under the guidance of the Holy Spirit received in tongues of flame at Pentecost. Thence the flame spread. First to the Jews, then, through Paul, to the Gentiles. Nothing could stop it. Persecution, strife, controversy, schism, corruption, ambition, wealth, power — each in turn threatened the gospel's end. But it continued to live on. At each sign of faltering there arose a new messenger to lift high the torch. Missionaries — martyrs and heroes —

planted the cross even to the north of Asia and in the far reaches of the British Isles. Northward, eastward, westward, southward, following the compass in its dizzy swinging toward man's discoveries and man's destiny. One hundred, two hundred, three hundred, five, ten, fifteen, nineteen hundred. Year after year, the ceaseless sharing and passing along from man to man, from age to age, from nation to nation, the " Good News," the infinite love, of the living Christ.

Voices (as before): He is not dead, He is risen.

Voice: He is alive today, now, this very minute, living for you and for every creature on earth. To His disciples He said " Come." To His disciples he said " Go." His disciples obeyed and the word was passed along to those who had not heard. Another link was forged in the chain of the ascending life. There was no rest, no pause, from proclaiming ceaselessly the message — the " Good News " — the wonderful, life-giving story of the Lord Jesus!

(Organ swells out as Prologue ends. Curtains will remain parted during entire performance. Also light on cross will remain plainly visible.)

Scene 1

(As organ dies away, the Voice comes from the cross.)

Voice: What of the disciples today? Dr. Grafton Burke, a disciple in Alaska, carries on.

(Lights come up. A spot left center on doctor, standing by outside plinth, leaning against it. Another spot on nurse, seated at right of center block.)

Nurse (looking up and seeing the doctor): Doctor Burke, what is the matter? You look sick.

Doctor: It is nothing. I'm just a bit shaky, perhaps. The child may die. We've done all we can but we are out of badly needed drugs and supplies. Jane, I'm heartsick. It seems that they have not cared enough about the work here. We're helpless without them. Do you think they've deserted us completely?

Nurse: Of course not, Doctor, they couldn't do that. Perhaps the next boat will bring those supplies and that much needed money.

Doctor: Yes, perhaps. I pray God it will. But that boat has come and gone so many times with nothing for us except letter after dreary letter, saying, " Sorry, no more funds."

Nurse (going over to the doctor): Doctor, you look so pale. Please come and sit down in this chair. Let me help you.

Doctor: I'm quite all right. Don't worry. I've had a hard day, that's all; and I've been wondering how we are going to care for all of our cases this winter. We lack the money to buy even the fuel to keep the patients warm.

Nurse: Don't be discouraged, Doctor. They are bound to send us help before long. They won't let your work of thirty years go for naught.

Doctor: Thirty years — a long time — but Christ wanted me here — perhaps this is the end of the journey. (Walks downstage.) My good friend Teusler has already passed on to the larger life. He builded well. He left behind a great hospital as a monument to his memory. He had a hard time, too. (Walks to corner of desk.) Perhaps things will turn out all right. I am ashamed to be discouraged and downcast like this. I, a Christian — But the boy — I'm sure he won't live. After thirty years I should be used to seeing people die, but never when it is needless — I want him to live. I want them all to live. I'd gladly give my life if that would help. (He sways, places his hand to his head. The nurse comes to help him.)

(As scene ends, choir sings very softly, " God so Loved

the World." This is followed by organ build-up to Scene 2
as Voice is heard.)

SCENE 2

Voice: St. Paul's Vestry considers the missionary appeal.

(Flood spot in center stage reveals rector seated to left
of center block. Vestrymen are grouped at right end, standing and leaning upon block.)

Senior Warden: But, Padre, we need the money so desperately here.

First Vestryman: After all, we need the money more than
they do.

Rector: Yes, I know. It's the same old argument every
year. The parish must come first. It has been even worse,
I think, since we've been allowed the privilege of saying
voluntarily what we would share for the spread of Christ's
kingdom. We'll pay what the church taxes us, even if
grudgingly, but we won't give.

Second Vestryman: That's all very well when we have
plenty of money and can spare it.

Rector: That's just it! We'll never have enough money
unless we dare to make a venture of faith once in a while.

Senior Warden: I wouldn't mind sending money to
foreign missions —

Rector: There is no such thing as " foreign missions," Jim.
We were " foreign " at one time ourselves. It's a mutual
thing, gentlemen, and we must shoulder our share of the
burden.

Third Vestryman: I'm inclined to agree with the rector.
He should know more about this thing than we do. Let's
leave the amount up to him.

Rector: Thank you, Kinkeid. I should like to set the
minimum all right, but we are all doing the giving. It must
come gladly from you.

Junior Warden: I'm afraid if we give too much to the quota, we can't manage that new roof this year as planned.

Fourth Vestryman: I hesitate to speak because this is my first experience with the budget. But it seems to me if the need is there and our share must be so much, there should be no question as to our response.

Senior Warden: I'd rather see the rector's salary raised and keep that money at home, if we must spend it.

Rector: What would a business man say to a proposition made to industry, to manufacturers, to merchants and to farmers that nothing made or raised in the United States was to be sold beyond the borders of the United States? Absurd, isn't it? We say " Yes " to steel and soap, chewing gum and cigarettes, automobiles and oil, while we say " No " to the greatest possession we have, the gospel of Christ. It simply doesn't make sense.

Fourth Vestryman: It all sounds logical to me. I see the rector's point and it makes me feel a little selfish. Perhaps we can cut down on something else if we find we have to, but I'm in favor of increasing the quota.

Fifth Vestryman: The increase is all right, but it still seems to me sort of foolish to send money to nations already pretty well supplied with religions.

Rector: Admittedly there are good points in all of these religions, but Christianity is the only one that faces life squarely and meets every need of mankind with some hope of solution.

Junior Warden: I think we've discussed this long enough. Someone make a motion.

Senior Warden: Very well, I move —

Rector: Just a moment. Remember what you're doing when you make that motion.

Senior Warden (after a brief pause): Yes, I know what I'm doing. I move that we give $100 toward the quota for next year.

Rector: I cannot accept such a motion. We must find a way to do our part, our full part.

(Organ swells out triumphantly as scene ends with brief interlude leading into opening of Scene 3, as the Voice is heard above chorus, singing in childish fashion, " Jesus loves me, this I know, for the Bible tells me so.")

SCENE 3

Voice: Two disciples in Liberia carry on.

(Chorus swells out as lights come up. Teacher is standing at right corner of block. Children are grouped, stair-step fashion, behind the block, standing.)

Teacher: Now, then, march out very quietly for morning recess.

(Children march out. Sounds of laughter heard all during the scene. Another teacher comes in.)

Another Teacher: A letter for you, Mary.

Teacher: I hope it contains better news than the last one from home.

Another Teacher: Hurry and open it.

Teacher (reads letter): Our budget has been cut again.

Another Teacher: But we couldn't keep the school open much longer on what we are already getting, and now, this.

Teacher: Yes, I know. It has been difficult enough during the past year, trying to exist and keep things going after that first big cut, without adding a second one to it.

Another Teacher: Our salaries have barely covered expenses, the necessities. Goodness knows, I didn't come out here to get rich, but I did expect to live decently.

Teacher: I am so weary of struggling on when the church at home can't even support me or encourage me. It doesn't take much. I came here for Christ's sake, not my own, but I would like to feel that the church is behind me.

Another Teacher: Why can't the church people at home see that we are working for them, doing their part? That we are merely their representatives, that they are working through us. Surely, they should be willing to give the money if we are willing to give our lives.

Teacher: It must be because they don't understand, not because they don't care. We can't close this school, you know that. This work must go on. We must stay, of course. These people need us. When I think of our bishop and priests toiling over jungle trails, trying so hard to meet the need, but unable to take full advantage of the many opportunities because time and strength and money will not permit, I become almost frantic.

Another Teacher: The chiefs in the interior, too, are begging for Christian teachers. They have heard that we are teaching these people to be both good Christians and good Africans. They understand, I think, that we are trying to conserve the good points of native tribal life while endeavoring to free them forever from the dark terrors that dominate their primitive religion.

Teacher: But there's no one to send them now. Simply because at home they are so far away that they cannot see as we see.

Another Teacher: Some day, perhaps, this little country may be able to provide for its own schools, its own church, but not yet. They haven't sufficient funds or ability or initiative now.

Teacher: Without our schools most of these girls would never learn to read and write; never learn at firsthand the word of God; never be able to pass it along by words spoken or written. We must show them, teach them, or they can never stand alone.

Another Teacher: They must be trained, Mary, if for no other reason than to rise above the ignorance and superstition of their ancestors — But we've work to do. I'll see you after school.

Teacher: All right, Gladys.

(Another Teacher exits. Sound of children singing swells up so that it can be heard plainly. Teacher ponders.)

Teacher: Christ wants them. I am his emissary. He has never deserted me. I'll never desert him. This work must go on, with money or without money. I still have faith in this continent of the future. (Children singing of God's love. Teacher bows head.) " Our Father —"

(As teacher begins to pray, chorus picks it up and swells into " Our Father " from the *Missa Marialis.* Organ continues and leads up to Scene 4 as Voice is heard.)

SCENE 4

Voice: The Every Member Canvass.

(Lights up. Mrs. Warren seated at left of block. Mr. W. is seated behind and in center of block. The canvassers stand at right end of block, a short distance away. Junior is seated in front of block, down center, looking at a book.)

Mr. W.: I think we understand about everything in the budget except that item labeled " Quota." Doesn't that mean " foreign missions " ?

First Canvasser: No, not at all. Just the contrary. You see, that goes for the missionary work in this diocese in places too small to support themselves. Also, for the missionary work in the United States. For example, the missionary district of North Texas gets $16,000 from the National Council. A comparatively small amount goes for what you call " foreign missions." Another example. Out of the $200 we are giving for the quota, some $125 remains in the diocese, about $40 remains here in the United States, while only the remaining $35 goes for work elsewhere.

Mr. W.: I don't believe in foreign missions. I don't want

any of my money going for that. I might as well be frank.

First Canvasser: You see, Mr. Warren, such a small amount of the entire budget, not quite 10 per cent, goes for the work I've just mentioned, and only a negligible amount of that leaves the United States at all. Your money, however, will be spent as you desire. That is your privilege.

Mrs. W.: We've heard so much about the mission field in our Auxiliary that I'm sold on it myself, but my husband doesn't see it yet.

Second Canvasser: That's quite all right, Mrs. Warren. I hope, though, you've both come to some decision about the amount of your pledge for the coming year.

Mr. W.: I guess you'd better put us down for the same amount as last year, with the understanding that it will all be spent here at home.

Junior (going over to his father, with the Sunday-school book which he has been studying diligently in his hand): Daddy, who is my neighbor?

(As lights fade quickly, the organ comes in to lead into Scene 5. The interlude must continue long enough to produce the atmosphere essential for next scene. The organ will be heard very faintly throughout entire scene.)

SCENE 5

Voice: A million lepers in China plead for Christian mercy. Sixty of these brothers fill to overflowing Nanchang Leprosarium.

(Lights up. Reveal a group of lepers in green spot grouped under arch, left center stage back, where missionary priest is standing on second step.)

Voices: Have mercy.

For Christ's sake, let us in.

Missionary: My brothers in Christ, be patient. We are filled to capacity; we can't let you in now; there is no more room. But we are begging for money with which to provide for you all. Won't you join your prayers to ours? I know we shall find a way.

Voices: We are unclean.

We are condemned.

Take our children.

Give them a chance.

No one cares what becomes of us.

Men despise us.

Missionary: No, no, my friends. God is not to blame nor is man. God loves each one of you. He will provide for you and for your children in time. Weep not now, but pray and keep the faith. The lands of Christ, when they hear, will send succor that you may live. Go in peace. God's blessings rest upon you.

(The crowd walks away very slowly and sadly. The missionary looks up to heaven for a moment, then turns to go.)

(Chorus sings an *Agnus Dei.* Organ continues and builds up mood for Scene 6. Voice is heard as organ ends abruptly.)

SCENE 6

Voice: St. James' Guild conducts its business.

(A group of women, half under each archway. President behind block center. Women engaged in knitting and sewing.)

First Woman: I think it's terrible about those poor Chinese starving to death. They seem to have something terrible happening to them all the time.

Second Woman: Why, I read the other day where in some places in China they put little babies out in the cold to die.

Third Woman: Tsk, tsk, tsk, tsk. That's a shame. Poor little things.

Fourth Woman: And they have those terrible lepers over there, too. Ugh!

Fifth Woman: I've seen pictures of those little children with puffed-out stomachs.

First Woman: That's from not having enough food.

Sixth Woman: Why doesn't someone over there do something about it?

Second Woman: I don't know, but someone should.

President (after arranging the papers on her table, raps for order): Quiet, please, ladies. The meeting will please come to order. There's a lot of work to be done. You know that rummage sale is coming off next week.

Third Woman: I've already thought of how cute we can fix up the rector's study with the money.

Fourth Woman: Don't anyone dare breathe a word, now. He thinks the money is going for the young people's party.

Fifth Woman: I know he'll be thrilled to death.

President: Who will handle the white elephant table?

(Organ interrupts with " Sleepers, Wake " [choral] with trumpet. Scene 7 follows immediately, at close of number.)

SCENE 7

Voice: The problem of missions turns up in the bishop's office.

(As lights come up, bishop and archdeacon are seated at center block. Bishop back and center; archdeacon right, at end.)

Bishop: It irks the layman to think of sending money to China or Japan or even Alaska, especially when he feels it is needed at home in his own parish or diocese.

Archdeacon: Even here, though, Bishop, in this diocese, we have fallen short. Look at our own struggling missions. Not enough men. Small pay for those we do have. More work than they can possibly do. Spreading themselves thinly over the large territory covered by two or three missions. And our people are neglected. I come across them every day. We must seek for support among the larger parishes, which are, as near as I can tell, not even interested in parochial or diocesan missions. Opportunities are being passed by with too little concern on our part.

(A missionary comes in unannounced.)

Missionary Clergyman: Hello, Bishop. Hello, Charles.

Bishop: Sit down, John. What can we do for you?

Missionary Clergyman: Well, Bishop, I'm discouraged. I can't be in all places at once and we're not doing the job adequately. For example, in Jacksonville. We've been so irregular there, with no church school, that all of our children are forced to go elsewhere for their Christian education. Also, their parents often attend the same churches because we have no morning service. We are grateful to these churches for doing our job. But that means a loss now and in the future. Can't you let me take one mission at a time and build it up?

Archdeacon: We were just discussing that, John. It wouldn't take long to show some fine results with just one place to handle. But these other places need you too, and we haven't the money to provide more men just now.

(Telephone rings. Bishop answers.)

Bishop: Hello — Yes — All right, put him on. — It's from Jasper. — Hello — Yes, Mr. Cartwright — yes — yes — Certainly. You arrange for a service there tomorrow morning at 11.30 and someone will be there. All right, we'll see you first. You're welcome. Good-by. It's old man Dagwell. They don't think he is going to get well. They want a last communion for him. Can you go, Charles?

Archdeacon (looks at date-book): I'm supposed to be in Conroe, Huntsville, and Trinity tomorrow, Bishop.

Missionary Clergyman: I'd go, Bishop, but I have services in Henderson tomorrow myself and I have no car.

Bishop: I'll go myself, although I can't spare the time. There's an example right there of one of the needs.

(A young college girl from Huntsville comes in. Secretary announces her.)

Bishop: Come in, Cynthia. Sit down.

College Girl: Oh, no, Bishop, I couldn't. I'm in a hurry. What I wanted to know was this: Couldn't you arrange for someone to take care of the school at Huntsville? We need someone badly. There are girls who want to attend the Episcopal church and can't. They'd be good missionaries when they get back home, too, Bishop.

Bishop: We'll see what we can do, Cynthia. Good-by.

Bishop: Talk about needs and challenging opportunities. As Christians, we shouldn't waste a minute seizing each one. We're handicapped because not enough of us have caught the vision. For the most part, we are not willing to share. Just to think, it took at least ten thousand men two thousand years of sharing Christ before any one of us could become a Christian.

Archdeacon: If only some of the larger churches —

(A visit from the building committee of a large parish interrupts the archdeacon's speech. A committee of three. One does the talking.)

Committee: Don't let us interrupt, Gentlemen.

Bishop: Come in, Mr. Smith. How are you, Mr. Dole, Mr. Andrews? You know these men, don't you? Mr. Sumners and Mr. Jones.

Committee: Oh, yes, how are you? We won't take but a minute of your time, Bishop. We want to get your approval of our plans for the new chapel. (Spreads plans out on desk.)

Bishop: How much will it cost?

Committee: About $5,000. It is very small, you know, but badly needed. You knew, also, of course, that we are getting an assistant.

Bishop: Do you know how much your parish pays toward the quota?

Committee: Why, no. I don't believe I do. But you see I am acting on this special committee only.

Bishop: Just $500, when it should be $4,000.

Committee: But, Bishop, I'm sure the Vestry will do more in time. At present we must get these important matters settled.

(Chorus sings all verses of " Thy Kingdom Come, O God." Organ as background during interlude.)

INTERLUDE

Voice: The fields are white unto the harvest. The ripened grain is being garnered by the faithful followers of Christ. The darkness of the world is being filled with glorious brightness. Disciples of all nations form the forward command — " Go ye " — " baptize " — " preach " — to all men. Fighting valiantly onward toward the goal of the kingdom. The noble army of " one-man." As the seasons of God become the seasons of man, the seed grows — there's more money, men, vision, turning, following, learning, praying, worshiping, serving, sharing. . . ."

(Organ modulates into chorus from Gounod's *Redemption,* followed by " Unfold, Ye Portals." Organ continues, as Voice announces the next scene.)

SCENE 8

Voice: Old Barnlett, the Scrooge of Christ.

(As lights come up, Old Barnlett is seated in center behind block. Stenographer is standing at left end of block.)

Barnlett: Are there any more letters, Miss Holland? Good, I'm ready to go home.

Office Boy: Sorry, Sir, but a gentleman to see you.

Barnlett: Who is it?

Office Boy: The Reverend Walter Meade, I believe, Sir.

Barnlett: All right, show him in. But it looks like these parsons don't have sense enough to know when to call.

Meade: Good-afternoon, Mr. Barnlett, and Miss Holland.

Barnlett: What do you want now? Sit down, but I shall have to ask you to make it brief.

Meade: I need your help, Mr. Barnlett. You are one of the more prominent members of the parish, with a little more money than the rest, perhaps. What I want is a donation toward the missionary work of the church. We are facing a large deficit. This would be a special gift, of course.

Barnlett: So you want a donation for missions, eh? Well, I won't give it. It doesn't do a bit of good. Pouring money into those far-away places. If I make any donation at all, it will be spent right here in this city. I've made my money here, and here it stays.

Meade: But you don't understand how badly it is needed. What a tremendous amount of good it would do.

Barnlett: Yes, yes. Sorry to disappoint you. (Meade starts to say something further.) No, I don't want to hear any more. Good-day! (Meade leaves — the secretary after him. Barnlett is alone.)

Barnlett: I'm not foolish enough to waste my money on those heathen. Let them alone. They've gotten along all right so far. (Yawns.) My, but I'm tired. (Lays his head on his desk as lights dim, leaving a faint glow from desk lamp.)

(As Barnlett sleeps, lights remain dim and organ carries mood.)

Voice: Out of the fabric of his dreamland, Old Barnlett weaves a picture new to his mind. He catches a glimpse of his rector's vision.

(Dim colored spot reveals characters for bits all grouped underneath the cross on top platform center. Pin spot brings out each character as he speaks. Organ sets the mood for each bit, with brief transition between. Barnlett remains dimly visible in foreground through entire scene.)

Minister (pleading for missions, spotted left): Christians cannot turn away from the cries of the world for help. These least of the world look to you for succor. You are their only hope of salvation. Inasmuch as you have or have not done unto these, so will your life be measured. Those cries of anguish will ring hauntingly in your ears forever, unless you hear and heed. Missions are, today, a vital necessity everywhere, the one sure way to cure ills, to answer needs, to take advantage of opportunities for service which are so manifold and obvious throughout the world. We must needs hasten to alleviate them all. Hear some of these crying needs, some of these opportunities, beckoning for you to come and see and do. (Music)

Displaced Person (emaciated, in tatters and filthy rags, with broken dialect): We are the fruit of war. We are war's end. But it has not ended for us. No home, no country, no family. Why can't we die? If only the Christian Church could reach out and touch us in our desperate plight. (Music)

A Woman of the Streets (dressed to arouse pity): I'm a victim of circumstance. I hate my filthy life. I'm a prisoner. There's no other way. God help me as his Son did that sister of mine, so long ago. Don't leave me in the red glare of the shadows. (Music)

A Flop-House Bum: We can't help our looks and the stench. We can't help that dumb look in our eyes. We're whipped and don't care much, anyway. There's nothing left, not even self-respect. There's no work. We are derelicts, moving from place to place, in the hope that something will turn up. It never does. Why do we have to be bums in the wealthiest nation in the world? A Christian nation. Our only hope lies in death — even then — (Music)

A Maimed War Veteran (horribly crippled): People ask me of war. My body is the answer. It took all and gave nothing. My buddies were the best God could create. They were slaughtered — wounded, like me — they were driven crazy — they were left to die — alone. Glory then, to save the world. But the nations still quarrel over rights and powers, and an organized world in which war is outlawed seems as far away as ever. (Music)

Chinese and Japanese Students (a group of five, three Chinese and two Japanese — the Chinese have come over to Japan to try to reach an understanding between the actions of the two nations on the strength of their mutual Christianity — one of the Chinese speaks): We are agreed. We have faith in God's power to solve our difficulties instead of relying on force. We shall bind ourselves now as Christians to attempt to settle all disputes between our nations in the future, seated around a table in the presence of Christ. We shall attempt to lead China and Japan tomorrow into the ways of understanding and peace. (All agree.) (Music)

E. Stanley Jones speaks for India: I have said to India: " I do not make a special drive upon you because you are the neediest people of our race, but because you are a member of our race. I am convinced that the only kind of world worth having is a world patterned after the mind and spirit of Jesus. I am therefore making a drive upon the world as it is, in behalf of the world as it ought to be, and as you are a part of that world, I come to you. But I would not be here an hour if I did not know that ten others were doing in the same land from which I come what I am trying to do here. We are all in the same deep need. Christ, I believe, can supply that need." (Music)

Kagawa (Kagawa and the raven of Elijah, as Kagawa is driven from the slums. The turning point in his life — Kagawa leaning on arm, raising himself up from the floor —

the raven stoops to help him.): They've driven me out. Why will they not accept my love? I give it freely. Maybe this is not the way. Oh, Raven of Elijah, what shall we do?

Raven: The kingdom of God movement. Now's the time to spread it throughout Japan. The co-operatives. Your industrial evangelism. This is the way out. You, Kagawa, must move out of the slums and into the world.

Kagawa: Co-operation in the name of Christ — for the whole world. That's it. We must remove the basic causes of slums and wars and social injustice before my dream can come true. That's what we'll do now, by the grace of God. Let us be on our way. The love of Christ will open the gates.

(As spots fade and spot on Barnlett comes up, Voice of Minister is heard above music.)

Minister: The great adventure of missions lies ahead for you. You, through your church, are creating Christ-spots in barren lands. The spirit of Christ is being made manifest. The spirit of the Twelve carries on — through and in you.

Voice (as lights come up and Barnlett awakes): Old Barnlett awakes from his dream. His vision has aroused his soul to action. Another " on the road to Damascus."

Barnlett: Was it a dream! It couldn't have been. It was so real. I have been an old fool. Never thought of it that way before. God forgive me. But it's not too late. I shall make that gift — and more — (Leaves desk, walks downstage. Suddenly a brilliant spot blinds him down center; he throws up his hands and murmurs — " God.")

(Organ goes into Gounod's " Sanctus " as spot fades on Barnlett and cyclorama parts on chorus with brilliant white spot from behind cyclorama and above chorus. As chorus diminishes to pianissimo on "Amen," the Voice is heard above the music.)

Epilogue

Voice: I'll make of all mankind one nation to dwell upon the face of the whole earth, saith the Lord.

Ye shall receive power and ye shall be my witnesses. . . . Go ye therefore and make disciples of all nations that they may know I came to give unto them a more abundant life.

Love one another — make wars to cease — banish hunger — and injustice — minister to the sorrowful and needy — and remember my commands — for, lo, I am with you always, even unto the end of the world.

(Curtain comes together slowly as cyclorama folds are lowered and the organ modulates into the " Hallelujah Chorus " from the *Messiah* as the organ postlude.)

If ideas can be dramatized and given strength to walk into lives otherwise closed to them, we should develop any latent gift for writing that we have, and present the results in whatever way seems best, whether an actual enacted play in the church, like " In the Night "; or a drama written to be read before a congregation in place of a sermon, like " Lonely Soul "; or a dramatic story written to be read by oneself or to others, like "A Dead Man Nailed to a Gaunt Bare Tree "; or a pageant big enough to present the world responsibility of the Christian Church.

" Every man heard them speak in his own language." To some, this speaking must be in dramatic form. Their interest must be caught before they will listen to what we have to say.

After the curtain falls some remembrance should remain, and the meaning of what was seen should come alive and walk into the scenes we play daily on the stage of life.

CHAPTER IX

RADIO: SERMONS
DRAMATIC STORIES

Yea, he did fly upon the wings of the wind.
PSALMS 18:10

MAY I REMIND you again that Dr. George A. Buttrick once admonished a summer clergy conference to use every avenue open for the spread of the good news, especially, " the written word in published form and *the voice over the radio*." All of us are being given increasingly the opportunity to " air " our sermons and services, and to give devotional talks and meditations over local radio stations. We must make full use of all these opportunities and not despise a single one. Too often we'll give a radio talk without proper regard for the medium. We preach as we would to a congregation before us. We write as we would for an audience we can see. Radio speaking is demanding and exacting. A manuscript must be painstakingly prepared and timed to the second, yet read without hurry, and without the stiffness which usually comes when we are chained to a page before us. The radio listener can turn us off at any moment. We must strive to hold all who tune in until the end. A warmed-over sermon or time-filling *ad libs.* will never win many to Christ.

After several years of continuous broadcasting, including a daily five-minute devotional period " Haven," a fifteen-minute " Church of the Air " Sunday program, and a fifteen-minute weekly story program, " Parson Jim," I submit a few samples which have worked well through the miracle medium of radio.

First, two examples of sermons written especially for the radio and used in no other way.

Mutual's Radio Chapel

" To give light to them that sit in darkness and in the shadow of death."

This arresting fact concerning the purpose of Christ's coming, from the Gospel of Luke, verse 79 of chapter 1, is at once the hope and the challenge of our daily life, and the grounds for Christian revolutions.

Mark well the passing years. The summer stars and the winter moon of the years just passed, " shook out pain and warning, strange laughters "[1] from men who must die; shook out blight and destruction for most of earth's people. " Life came and went and there were men and women who seemed to have been candles lighted and to be seen, 'til a sudden gust of wind had come and their lights no longer met the eyes; they had been; they no longer were." [2] This is the story of too many war years that have passed into the limbo of forgotten things. The age-old gust of wind sweeps away with the passing years all that is not anchored well or sunk deep.

Mark well the years to come, which begin like a match just struck, its flame still sputtering and wavering, as if it were not certain of itself. We wonder: Shall we be able to hold it steady till the flame burns sure; will it burn long enough to light a light of longer burning, or will it scorch our fingers and go out as we drop it, and leave us in deeper darkness?

In my imagination I see the match light a lamp in the hands of a wise old man. He carefully adjusts the flaming

---

[1] From *Abraham Lincoln, The Prairie Years*, by Carl Sandburg, Vol. I. Harcourt, Brace and Company, Inc. Used by permission.

[2] *Ibid.*

wick and covers it against the wind and holds it high as he stalks hurriedly away in his search for maturity; he is restless, a bit impatient; he does not pause. What will this old man, this seeker of maturity, find when his lamp shines upon us — one of you, or me? Will he find " laughter and youth in your bones, in your heart a few pennies of dreams, in your head a ragbag of thoughts you could never expect to sell " [1] or maturity, possessed of sight and insight, having " a right judgment in all things " ?

All we ask of that flimsy flaming match of the years is that it will burn long enough for us to see and to recognize our own immaturities, to gaze at them long enough to despise them and to want maturity, and before it flickers out, to give some indication of the way to turn for ending our search, the old man's search for maturity ended in us. We hold the match. With it we must light a wick of longer burning and be found in its flame. The years are in our hands.

Well might this search for maturity be our supreme task for the rest of the year. We are childish in so many ways: our emotions and feelings and attitudes are far from grown-up, and we spend much of our time evading reality as it approaches. But the most sinister way in which we manifest our immaturity is our taking for granted the one thing that leads to complete maturity (and by taking it for granted we discount it altogether), and our surface thinking and acting on the greatest open secret in the world. I refer to Jesus Christ. How casual we are about him and how superficially we take the message of his religion — Christianity!

Know ye not that Christ is God's message of salvation to men? Yes, I know this is too good to be true, his coming

[1] From *Abraham Lincoln, The Prairie Years,* by Carl Sandburg, Vol. I. Harcourt, Brace and Company, Inc. Used by permission.

from the mind back of the universe, the eternal, just for us, just to show us the way. But it is true. It is like the brilliance of a western sunset which artists dare not attempt to capture on canvas, revealing the true brightness and purity of the colors as they actually are in nature. They are fearful no one will believe such radiant colors exist at all. The truth of the Incarnation is stranger than fiction. No man's mind could have conceived it. It is as impossible to the mind of man as the perfect crime. In this creation of God, however, in Christ and the meaning of his life and words, is no flaw at all.

If we only believed it, life would be wonderful, and the flame would not so much as flutter. The purpose of life would be known to us. Maturity, which is the possession of vision and understanding, would be ours. Yet this knowledge has been available for almost two thousand years, a direct answer for man's incompleteness, for his need of knowing how to live, for his peace and joy within, for his wearing not the mantle of darkness, but of light, the very garment of praise. Act this way, God says through Christ — certain things will follow. Act another way — certain other things will follow. It is all clear and plain for those who want to know, for those who really care.

If we only believed! Yet history proves the message to be straight and true. We have tried other ways and gotten results, such as having arrogance and greed bring their own kind of hell back upon us. He has told us so.

If we only believed it, then to mingle with other kindred Christian minds in order to learn more, and to help plan with them for pushing on to every soul who has not heard the message, would be life's centrality.

" Jesus Christ was either the Son of God or the world's biggest liar," so said a saintly scholar — a mature man. Surely we do not believe Jesus was the latter! And if we believe he was the Son of God — like God, aye, God himself — telling us which way to go, letting us see into the mind of the universe and learn how its laws work — why, what are we waiting for?

A solid look at the reality of the actual on this Sunday brings sad reports of lacks and lags and black shadows. Is it true what a great English clergyman said recently: " Over-shadowing all else is the vast ebbtide of religious faith " ? Many would say yes. But a solid look at the reality of the *possible* brings the kind of stir within that is born of hope and a future within reach. Jesus Christ is the sum and sub-stance of both hope and future. He came " to give light to them that sit in darkness and in the shadow of death." Christ is Christianity, and when we grow up, we realize that Christi-anity is not a set of principles, nor a system of ethics, nor a series of good examples. Christianity is a covenant, a per-sonal relationship with God; it is conformity to God's laws, obedience to God's commands, living under God's judgment as well as God's mercy.

Take this Jesus, Son of Man, Son of God. He was not simply a good man nor merely the best man. When I think of what men have done to him, I cringe and am sad. No! Christ was not Swinburne's " Pale Galilean " nor Dewey's humanistic Jesus of progressive education fame. He is God *and* man — never forget it. That is why we reverence the Incarnation, when God " became flesh and dwelt among us."

A man once gave a book review of a Life of Christ. The result was a picture (not the author's, incidentally, but the reviewer's own) of just another good man, a kindly teacher; and the tragedy of it was that everyone lauded the reviewer for the excellent job he had done, even though the real Jesus had been completely emasculated. Jesus as good ex-ample is not enough. Too often we feel like the mother of

the bad boy who had a good little cousin. Somehow all the
mother's admonishments to be good like the cousin had no
effect whatsoever. To say " be like Jesus " is not enough.
This is making him a purveyor of good advice and not a
proclaimer of good news. This is making his words lovely
ideals and goodly principles, instead of what they really are,
the ringing words of God's judgment, the code of the living
God for those who accept the challenge of his way. Remember the disciples were powerless until Pentecost. They
had been with Jesus, but only when his spirit possessed and
controlled them did people *take knowledge* that they had
been with him. Note that after this inner fire was kindled,
the wavering flames of the apostles became steady, burning
witnesses, emerging from the ashes of a consumed self.
Nothing was impossible now because the good example,
Christ, had become a *Savior* to whom they were welded
through repentance and forgiveness, and through whom the
faith and love and power of God began to pour in endless
torrent.

Yes, it was possible now to forgive seventy times seven,
for identification with Christ was complete. They had
achieved oneness, not merely likeness; they were in personal
covenant relationship with him, not following the inspirer
of good resolutions, but becoming co-partners with one
who led spiritual revolutions along the path of the world's
redemption. These Christians did turn the whole world
topsy-turvy, for a new light had begun to shine upon the
pages of history; and man's life, in the spotlight of Christ's
spirit presence, could no longer hide in the darkness of evil
ways, could no longer compromise with or out-argue God's
laws, could no longer water down the demands and commands of God for those who dwell in his universe.

Because of Jesus, man can no longer ignore or evade God.
He must either accept or reject him. He must either cover

up his bad conscience and sense of lack by refusing to acknowledge them, or let his pride be smashed through repentance, so that the chasm caused by following his own way to some form of self-centeredness may be closed, and the rebellion he has participated in by denying God's laws and refusing to obey them may cease. In short, we must confess the failure of our attempt to defy the infinite with the puny resources of the finite. The closing of the gap between man's life without God and man's life with God is possible when we want forgiveness, and when we accept the revolution we need to substitute for every good resolution. Such an experience is very much like walking into a revolving door, fastly spinning, and coming out on the other side, heading in a new direction with a new set of sights and insights.

If our Christian witness is just a set of good resolutions, and not a radical change of life from the usual dust and stone, it means we do not want to repent, do not want forgiveness, do not want the holiness of God.

My little boy said to me several times while we were setting up the manger scene under our Christmas tree, "But where is the *man* Jesus?" Somehow he knew there must be a man to complete the story of a baby, that there must be a time to put aside the immaturities of babyhood and to become a man, no longer talking like a child or thinking like a child or reasoning like a child or acting like a child. This tremendous act of Jesus' birth, of Incarnation, took shape in a baby who grew to maturity — completely man as God fashioned him to be. To think that this message, which so fills our lives at Christmastide, is a living and direct message from God! And yet we largely ignore it, ignore him as God, remain immature Christians.

It has been said that we want Christianity without God, without Christ, because we cannot stand in the presence

of God and say, " I'm good." That is why they crucified
Christ. That is why we crucify him. We are not yet willing
to accept his demands of repentance and new life. But when
we accept Christ, resolutions become revolutions, and the
freedom and peace of real maturity begin to dawn.

The world is not yet at an end in this " night of the Spirit "
save as the world of evil shakes beneath the vision of the
cross, this magnificent mystery which stands high and lu-
minous above a dark world; charging us with the inescapable responsibility for coming to repent and going with
forgiveness, to proclaim as fact the indwelling love of Christ,
which makes all the old deeds, so long fraught with fears and
uncertainties, all ashine with the great light we have seen
and have put around us as the sign of our captivity to Christ.

With Christ to the fore, our resolutions (so powerless to
do anything) will become revolutions (which means we
have turned around and are heading in a new direction)
resulting in the maturity of Christian realism. Christianity
is Jesus Christ and him alone. He is the central truth of the
universe. Wist ye not?

Mark well the passing years. Will their ends be like the
sorrowful sighing chorus of the song sung so mournfully for
years long gone, or will their music be a loud and victorious
chorus of the light which is Christ — a light sufficient for
those who sit in darkness and in the shadow of death to find
their way into the life of peace within and peace throughout
the world? It all depends on our maturity — on the match
we hold and what we light with it — a wisp of straw or a
fuse to a spiritual bomb that will blast us and the world into
a new life.

Steady with the light — the wind blows strong — the wick
is short — the flame is so small. Be quick to light the fuse
which turns as it burns, to explode " good resolutions " into
world-shaking revolutions through Christ.

Mark ye well this year. Will it contain more or less of
the light which is Christ, for us and for others through us?
Only ye can tell.

The Episcopal Hour — Depths

Text: Launch out into the deep. Luke 5:4

Part I. Depths — the innermost part of anything.

Life runs deep, often beyond our comprehension. The
sorrows of earth plunge sharply into our hearts. "A world
in ferment" is still an unresolved hurt in the soul of man.
England is as near hopeless as any undestroyed and un-
defeated nation can be. Palestine's endless tragedy swirls
around our feet. Russia's stubborn " no's " to the proposed
solutions for world confusion keep us fretful and anxious.
Science is running against itself in a race to keep monsters
from being masters, and we are fearful of the end. Men are
still as distrustful of each other as ever, for military victory
has not brought freedom from fear.

Yes, life runs deep, often beyond our comprehension.
T. S. Eliot's poem, *The Wasteland*, describes the picture
accurately. " We are hollow men. We are stuffed men.
Headpiece filled with straw." Shallow men, unfamiliar with
the deep and abiding things of life. Immature men, in whom
life's human potential is only about one-third or less developed. Hollow men, to whom life has become a hollow
tree, a place in which to hide.

We must watch the depths of confusion and dreariness all
around us by penetrating to the innermost part of them and
of ourselves and finding God there. We must trade hollow-
ness and emptiness for soundness and abundance. But how?
What *can* we do? Jesus gave the answer one day in a few
words he spoke to Peter, James, and John, as they washed
their nets after a fruitless night of fishing. Jesus stepped

into their boat and said, "Launch out into the deep." They
obeyed, reluctantly, and Jesus led them to a new casting
place — in deep water. A miraculous draught of fishes re-
sulted. The lesson is still there to be learned: launch out
into deep water under Christ's directive, keep casting deeper
and deeper until you make your catch, whether it be new
life, more light, forgiveness, successful world government,
or the courage to stand in the face of reality — whatever
satisfies our need and our brother's too.

The words still apply to all who are content to sway with
the tide, anchored in the mud like some old piling, going
no place, afraid of life and death, rotting away uselessly.
The command, "Launch out into the deep," gives us a clue
for Christian behavior today in a world struggling to release
itself from the shallows, trying desperately to find the strong,
foundational depths of hope and unshakable faith.

This word of God through Christ, when obeyed, means
redemption for our time from darkness and despair. The
Master speaks: "Launch out into the deep." We must obey
in faith.

Part II. Revelation — all we can know of God.

God is always attempting to reveal himself to man. But
man has ever been slow to perceive the light and the truth
opening to him. Witness the long centuries of the slowly
perceived revelations of God's nature until finally, almost
seemingly as a last resort, God revealed himself in Jesus
Christ to all men who would look at him and believe. This
was as specific a revelation of himself as God could make.
No longer was he some seemingly indefinite spirit, floating
above the earth like a cloud puff, but a flesh and blood being,
a person, a man; revealing all of himself man could understand.

The depths of God, long hidden, were at last revealed

forever in Jesus Christ. Upon this is based step number one in our launching — know the Christ. Man's long-continued disobedience and arrogance have distorted his vision of God. Until he opens his eyes in God's presence and sees himself for what he is, he will never turn and be saved from his human impotence.

God speaks through his Son. "Hear ye him." He that has seen the Son will know the Father. "Seek ye him." Do these things and you will find the innermost part of God revealed.

This story is told of Holman Hunt before he painted his famous picture, "The Light of the World." He told a friend, "I'm going to paint Christ." — "But you can paint only what you can see," the friend replied. — "But I'm going to see him. I will work by his side in the carpenter shop. I will walk with him over the hills of Galilee. I will go with him among the poor, the blind, the lame, and the leprous. I will go to Gethsemane with him. I will travel with him to Calvary and climb the cross with him, until I see him. And then I will paint him."

The innermost part of Christ is ready to open to all who desire him enough. "Sir, we would see Jesus." "Come and see" with your own eyes the things which have been revealed. This first. What then? The poignancy of John's words, "He came unto his own and his own received him not" (John 1:11), must be met by John's own cure, "But as many as received him, to them gave he power to become the sons of God." (John 1:12)

Part III. Perception — all we can understand and retain of God.

God revealed himself through his Son, so that men might more readily perceive his earth way for human life. But perceiving must merge into receiving his leadership before any permanent life change occurs. That is step number two. This is a hard depth to launch into for many. Especially those whose minds are hardened by preconceptions or whose thinking has been warped by conflicting authorities. When men find truth and fail to accept it, they are usually afraid to follow where it may lead, afraid of plumbing such depths, of questioning too far, of seeking ultimate truth, of learning about their real selves by coming close to God. They are fearful of awakening from their dreams to something demanding and real. These are top-water Christians, insensitive to God's yearning love for them, content with the mucky shallows.

Flash opinions, quick divorces, fancy fads, new religions — like existentialism, communism, and intimism; easy discouragement, idle gossip — all these are signs of shallow thinking and selfish living and the need for obeying Christ's command to " launch out into the deep."

The solid men like Arnold J. Toynbee, who has plumbed the depths of history and found hope, and the late Archbishop Temple, who plumbed the depths of theology and found certainty, go deeper and touch reality, and tap the resources of God's power.

The revelation brings awareness of the needs of self. Perception gives motivation to the acceptance of all of Christ in all of us; gives us courage to venture into deeper water. No matter how skilled or proficient we are, we need to add a new faith, like the disciples, who trusted Jesus' word, accepted it as a command, obeyed even though it seemed to repeat a failure.

The word of redemption lies deep and we must stay with it until we comprehend its meaning for us now. This means propinquity to Christ and his word; reading about him from the biblical record and pondering the meaning of his life for us; poring daily over his words, asking for the grace and wisdom to understand and the courage to follow whatever specific directions come.

The touch of Jesus' hands *once* upon our eyes is not enough. Accepting him in part or for a moment is not enough. The hem of his garment brushing us as he passes is not enough. The second touch, the full identification and oneness with him, still must happen, before God's revelation and man's perception have united into full-blown discipleship, with roots deep enough to hold him upright when hurricanes blow.

Hang onto Christ's words, begin to step along his way, respond to God enough to make headway into the depths of our need, which is the world's need in miniature, and keep moving until the word of redemption has wrought a complete change in us. New life in the innermost parts of us. That is what we call regeneration and step number three.

Part IV. Regeneration — using revelation and perception for the conduct of life.

Letting God have his way with us and becoming a new creature — this is the process of regeneration. It is living with the revelation and the perception until inner change occurs, until solid certainty and evidences of the abundant life appear in hollow men who were " full of fancies and empty meaning."

Why should there be a discouraged clergy and people in England? Why should the subject of unity be so flimsily conceived and stubbornly refused? Largely because depth regeneration has not yet come to most who were signed by the cross at baptism as " Christ's faithful soldiers and servants." When one experiences the joy which comes in redemption and the release from life's strains, tensions, worries, fears, and all such preconversion conditions, one can understand the relaxation and freedom of the river-boat pilot which come when the singsong cry of " Mark Twain " is heard above the churning and straining of the side-paddles over the dangerous shallows, into deep water.

What to do? Simple enough to tell: wash out the past and make up for it as best you can, as God directs; check your subsequent course daily in his presence: "to always pray" until attitudes are really changed, until the colors of our inner life become deep and rich and unfading; constant devotion to his word, listening in order to hear him speak; under discipline to his will, to obey his commands; to worship, ready to respond, ready to serve, to come into his presence humbly and go with his Spirit valiantly.

John said man must "be born again from above." That is, Christ must become our all in all and not simply a nodding acquaintance. When we really submit to God's way of law and love, as Jesus revealed, the innermost part of us will be touched and controlled by his life, and we shall *really* believe and act as if we believed that love is better than hate, magnanimity better than resentment and self-interest; and the promises of God will be fulfilled.

The Sermon on the Mount pictures the way of regeneration in between the positive promises of the Beatitudes and the solid conclusion of the house built upon the rock of conviction and obedience — " and digged deep, and laid the foundation on a rock." (Luke 6:48) Dive deep into these teachings of Jesus for guidance in living the regenerated life.

Unless we become part of this process of regeneration, the tides now gathering to sweep the earth will flick us from our moorings. "By their fruits ye shall know." What we are will be the evidence that we have known the Master and obeyed his command.

Part V. Evangelism — passing along what we have found that works.

The "word of redemption" lies deep down within men. God's dynamic word becomes articulate and powerful for the world, in the world, through the influence of the Holy

Spirit. But this disturbing and compelling inner power must find its expression in person-to-person contact by the regenerated Christian, and in the fearless fellowship of the church before the word of redemption for the individual becomes the way of salvation for the world.

With the river-boat pilot, we want to pass along the cry "Mark Twain" to the other boats stranded on the mudbanks with the deep channel so near. Telling others of these things we have learned and experienced may lead them to newness of life. Never cease growing, never stop telling. "When thou art converted, strengthen thy brethren." Luke (22:32)

The Church has the potential power to save the world from its trust in weak and fallible human nature alone. The failures of the dark nights of man's fishing can be redeemed as we continue to keep in living contact with Christ. This do, while at the same time reaching out to touch men and their needs by the wisdom and power of love which he would disclose through those who have been with him, those to whom the miracle has happened.

People are queer. We must be patient and understanding. People are so desperate they go berserk before our faces. We must be controlled. We have all seen the terrible unhappiness of men — yes, we can remember our own. That is why the word of "evangelism" is pointing us all to a task of immeasurable importance — no longer baiting for the fish of bazaar and barbecue, good works and nice people, comfortable budgets and cozy pews; but casting our nets for men, their bodies *and* souls.

The wonders from the depths of even this miserable and hungry world are waiting for Christian fishermen to cast their nets according to Christ's command and direction and bring in a miraculous draught of fishes. But never forget, only as the fishermen obeyed Jesus' directions, did they catch fishes *or* men. The Church's program of evangelism will fail unless this is remembered and applied. For this work Jesus wants keen and consecrated workmen who at his bidding, even though they have fished all night or all their lives and caught nothing, are ready to " launch out into the deep " and try again at his word of command. Without Christ all our work will go for naught. With Christ the harvest will be abundant.

Part VI. Conclusion — what we would carry away and apply.

Our orders for this unhappy year come from Jesus Christ our Lord. We must obey.

" Launch out into the deep," then, out into " a world in ferment," but with " the word of redemption " upon our lips, proclaiming allegiance to Christ as the way of salvation for men. And even as we speak with joy and conviction may our witness be made more compelling by the very manner of our speaking and the level of our living under the power of his Spirit.

*   *   *

Two selections from the fifteen-minute weekly series known as *Parson Jim*, depicting episodes in the eventful life of an ordinary minister.

Parson Jim and Sin

Parson Jim chuckled to himself over the clerical cartoon he came across in a magazine while waiting his turn in the barber shop. It showed a sweet young thing shaking the hand of her parson as she left the Sunday-morning service, and the caption told the story. Said the young lady to the rubicund clergyman: " I never knew about sin until you became our pastor." But as Parson Jim looked at the men in the barber chairs and listened to the hubbub of conversation, he knew the subject of the cartoon was no laughing matter. Sin was a nasty little word with the "*I*" squarely in the middle, descriptive of the prevalent condition of nearly every human life. But it was not popular to talk about sin. The word was too direct, too indecent sounding. Far better in this modern age to say "mistake" or "shortcoming."

The shine boy was calling, "You're next, Reverend." He was fortunate enough to get his favorite barber, Joe Stackler. The barber braked the chair and greeted Parson Jim.

"What's new, Doctor?"

Parson Jim replied instantly, "Sin." He smiled. "Not new exactly, Joe, but the word is new to many good people today. Did you know the Greeks did not have a single word for sin? But they had five words, each one telling something we ought to know *about* sin, which means to us doing something we ought not to do, a disobedience to some law."

"You don't say." Barber Stackler was the one who usually initiated the conversation, sometimes to Parson Jim's boredom. But today, the tongue was wagging in the other cheek.

"Do you want me to give you a lecture?" Parson Jim thought of the many world problems Joe had aired and solved to the snipping of scissors. He hoped his friend Stackler would listen.

"Sure, go ahead. It'll probably do me good." He whirled the chair for better light, jacked it up an inch or two, and then with legs spraddled, comb in one hand and scissors in the other, settled down to listen.

"Those five words are among the few I remember from my New Testament Greek. It is always helpful for an understanding of any word to trace it back to its roots. Here they are:

"The first and oldest one is ἁμαρτια. It was a term used in the very popular sport of archery. It means literally ' to miss the mark, the target.' The second one is παραβαινω, which means ' to go along a way ' or ' to get on the wrong road.' Another form of the word is sometimes used, παραβασις, ' the wrong direction of your going.' See, Joe, how easy it is to get the implication of these words? "

Joe stopped snipping for a moment, started to say something, changed his mind, and resumed his comb and scissor duet with, " What about the other three words? "

" Well another one is παραπιπτω, which is most expressive. It means ' to fall down from sheer weakness.' The most beautiful sounding one is the fourth one, a word for the musician, πλημμελεω, ' to be out of tune ' or ' a sour note.' The last one is probably the most descriptive, however, for us today. It is ακαθαρσια, which means ' impurity ' or ' one who doesn't fit ' or ' one without the necessary qualifications.' One who is not fit, medically, must be purified. This term is really for the artist and his profession and it comes from the same root. An artist is one who fits things together properly. But a sinner is one who has serious lacks in the art of fitting things together perfectly. In other words, Joe, religion is more than an affair of self with God; it is an affair of humanity and God, in which we must fit first with humanity. You see, every one of these words expresses a peculiarly human quality or occupation which prevents one from fulfilling his potential oneness with God."

" That makes some sense, Doctor, but why does the Christian Church teach that every man is a sinner since Adam — ' since Adam's fall, man sinnéd all,' as somebody said; and what about original sin? " Joe Stackler was acting in a new role of questioner seeking answers, rather than an infallible authority giving them.

Parson Jim went on:

" First I can tell you what we mean by the term ' original sin.' It is the tendency buried somewhere in our natures to make perverse or wrong choices, largely because we are born self-centered. Sin, all sin, is choosing something wrong because there is something desirable in it for us. Take the ancient story of Adam and Eve, which contains a very great truth. Not long ago I visited the archaeological museum of the University of Pennsylvania in Philadelphia. In one of the class display cabinets I found an old Assyrian clay tablet dating from about 1800 B. C. There, in picture form, is the story of Adam and Eve. The tree is there, the serpent, the apple, and the persons. But there are no words. However, the story is clear. Do you remember those words of the serpent to Eve, as he encouraged her to eat the apple? " Joe shook his head. He had not read the Bible in a long time, especially the Old Testament. " He said, ' ye shall not *surely* die,' meaning of course, ' come on and take a chance, you may get away with it.' Well, we've been trying to beat the rap of cause and effect ever since, hoping that wrong choices will not bring their inevitable consequences. We do not want to learn that disobedience to any law, natural or spiritual, brings finally its own punishment. But I'm afraid I'm preaching you a sermon."

The small shop had become still and Parson Jim found the only voice at work was his own and the only words heard above the work noises of the shop were his. All of them were listening to his discourse on sin. Even the elderly shine " boy " was refraining from smacking his rag against well-shined leather, easing it back and forth silently as he, too, listened. Parson Jim was a bit embarrassed. He had not meant to get on such a long subject. He thought perhaps he'd better look at his magazine, which was still open in his lap to that clerical cartoon. But the man in the next chair had a question.

" Oh, Reverend, excuse me, but what can one do about sin? "

The parson could hardly believe his ears. He plunged into the answer before the spell was broken.

" I'm glad you asked that question. The Christian religion, the Christian Church, seeks to save men from those things that are keeping them from God and offers forgiveness to every penitent sinner. That's the good news. Selfishness is at the root of all sinning — remember the ' I ' is always in the middle of every instance of sinning. Forgiveness is the answer. Forgiveness means to give force to one's seeking after God, but it does not mean escaping the consequences of one's sins — these follow as night does the day. Forgiveness means putting the wrong thing out of one's life, that which keeps us from God — adultery, pride, vainglory, hypocrisy, and all the rest. Back to the Greek. There is one Greek word for forgiveness and it means literally ' to drive out or send away.' But forgiveness comes only through the process of repentance, which is literally conversion. The steps in proper order are: Change your mind, face in the opposite direction, and move in that direction. Do I make myself clear? "

" Yes, Sir, almost too clear."

Parson Jim continued, " To sum it all up," for Joe was about finished, " sin with the ' I ' in the middle and God nowhere in evidence, makes us miss the mark, get on the wrong road, fall down, be out of tune, and unfit for human association. Salvation is the opposite and comes through Jesus Christ. We read in the Bible this promise, ' If any man sin, we have an advocate with the Father, Jesus Christ, the righteous.' (1 John 2:1) We also find in the same place these comforting words, ' Christ Jesus came into the world to save sinners. . . ." (1 Timothy 1:15) to help them hit the mark, to keep them on the right road, to strengthen them to withstand temptation, to harmonize their natures, to fit them into the scheme of the universe; and all these things according to God's plan."

As Parson Jim put on his collar, vest, coat and hat and reached for his billfold, he had one last remark for Joe alone. "You know, I believe the only way out of sin and entrance into a new life for any man is identification with Christ. This is a second, spiritual birth which pulls us up and out of ourselves."

Parson Jim tossed a tip to the shine boy for some expert whisking and gave a great big smile and good-by salute to the first barber-shop congregation he had ever known. He stepped onto the street. The air felt good. He had been so carried away with the experience in the barber shop he forgot for the moment his next objective. That really didn't matter; but what would come of his barber-shop interlude did. Could it be that any one who heard would remember and be benefited? He prayed that his witnessing might find lodgment in at least one man's heart and work the miracle of changed direction to his going. Parson Jim vowed to himself to make more out of all such opportunities for speaking a good word for the Lord Jesus.

Parson Jim learned later, to his great joy, that the man who asked the question in the next chair to his had heard the good news in time for it to influence a difficult decision in favor of God's way and not his own, and to give him the necessary impetus to go back to his own church, which he had left years before.

So the life of Parson Jim was lived from day to day, and the high moments of such incidents as we have recounted tonight held him ever closer to the Master he had chosen to follow.

Parson Jim Writes a Sermon Under the Clouds

The moonlight on the solid floor of clouds was a sight to enjoy and treasure. Parson Jim gazed out through the small

cabin window beyond the moon-drenched wing tip of the
DC-4 and felt that the magic carpet of ancient fable had
come true. Flying above the clouds in the moonlight was a
wonderful and rare experience for Parson Jim. Sarah did
not like him to fly, since just a year or so before their
marriage he had been seriously injured in the crash of the
plane he was piloting. But this trip was necessary in order
to arrive on time for an important engagement. Thoughts
of accident were far from him, as the small red glow from
the exhaust pipe of the near motor and the beauty of the
slowly passing cloud mass kept him close to the window and
far from reality.

A visit with a sick parishioner the week before had given
Parson Jim a new phrase which seemed to write itself across
the heavenly space stretched far beyond, — "A talk with
the Man upstairs." His parishioner had meant his close brush
with death, and how he had just missed the opportunity to
see his Maker face to face. But to Parson Jim it had been a
wonderful phrase to describe prayer. He was always on the
lookout for phrases and illustrations for sermons. He looked
again at the clouds below and felt secure in the warm cabin
of the plane. But it occurred to him how often preaching
was high up, above the clouds, so far beyond the listeners
that their accurate description, " It was over my head," applied. When Parson Jim flew for fun, one of his favorite
moments was to fly just under the cloud ceiling, with the
clouds so close above he could reach out and scoop down
the moisture. This was the way a sermon ought to be —
high and lifted up, but not lost in the clouds.

He was becoming cramped and uncomfortable with his
face glued to the window for so long a time, and he was
growing a bit chilly. So he got the attractive stewardess to
tuck a blanket around his feet. He settled back, turned on
the small pin spot above the seat, pulled out his sermon notes

for next Sunday on " Christian Duty " and began to read,
determined to keep the content under the ceiling of the
congregation's understanding.

The Text: Let us hear the conclusion of the whole matter.
Fear God, and keep his commandments: for this is the whole
duty of man. (Ecclesiastes 12:13)

The Introduction: No cow can say, " I want to be a better
cow." Only man can desire to be better.

It is a man's duty, his Christian duty certainly, to want to
be a better man.

Only human beings can have a sense of duty. And yet
how wearying for human beings to hear: " It's your duty ";
" You ought to do this or that or the other thing."

But that " ought " is essential, for it is part of the process
of attaining a desired end. Duty is that which we do from
choice because we desire a certain end. We don't have to do
certain things. We are compelled only by the end desired.

A music student doesn't have to practice — unless he wants
to be a musician.

A traveler doesn't need to hurry to catch a train — unless
he wants to reach his destination.

A motorist can ignore signposts — unless he doesn't want
to get lost.

If we want to be better we ought, it is our bounden duty,
to do certain things. The obligation is immediate; the responsibility is inescapable.

I assume we are human beings desiring to achieve a higher
level of living, wanting to do our duty — our Christian duty.

Part I. The text says—" Fear God and obey him." Rather
fear the result of our choice to disobey him.

The Christian ideal, which it is our duty to desire and
seek after, has an absolute standard which we find in the

Decalogue and Sermon on the Mount, and makes infinite demands as catalogued in the seven virtues.

The Church holds the guide map to the Christian way. Lecky calls it " the map of life," which is already prepared — the road leading to the Christian ideal, which we ought to take, because only by so doing can we get to the place of the abundant life.

There are several major premises which we must assume: (1) the belief in God as Creator, Judge, Redeemer, Incarnate in Jesus Christ, who gives men grace and power by the Holy Spirit; (2) freedom of human will, that man can choose good or evil; (3) man cannot achieve the ideal by his own efforts, he is not self-sufficient; (4) the soul has a natural tendency to seek God, to perceive what is good and right.

We can turn now to an examination of the Christian ideal as summarized in the Christian virtues, after which we'll seek to apply them to one or more specific cases of conscience.

Part II. Virtue has to do with regulating self for remote ends, and is peculiar to human beings. Cows may be contented but never virtuous. Virtue requires effort to develop and is only potential until developed; and this development involves knowledge and choice.

There are two kinds of virtues: cardinal, which can be developed by man alone; spiritual, which can be developed only by God's help and grace. Only a Christian can possess the latter; any good man can develop the former. The Christian must develop the cardinal virtues, but it is the fruits of the spirit, which we can learn only by individual effort *and* God's help, that mark us off as Christians.

Note briefly the cardinal virtues:

Justice — rightness over against wrongness—giving everyone his due, even the devil.

Prudence — decisions for remote ends — referring all questions to the criterion of God's will for us.

Temperance — self-control for highest ends.

Fortitude — deliberate bravery — the spirit which resists and endures, and even triumphs over the trials and temptations of life.

Anyone can work these into his life, can become a self-made man.

But the spiritual virtues, called so because they alone lead to the vision of God, are given by God alone and are concerned with the end of life. They appeal to our better natures.

Faith — deliberate trustworthiness — being absolutely dependable.

Hope — desire and expectation of God's good ends for life and beyond.

Love — inflexible devotion. Taking responsibility. Willing to give or give up anything.

But of what value to living are these masses of ideals held up before us as a far-off goal? What of immediate applications? So, some cases of conscience.

(Parson Jim paused again and began pondering. His second point was too succinct. It had too many enumerations and not enough windows. He needed one or two good illustrations. The plane hit a down draft of air and dropped suddenly, finding solid air again in a moment with a jarring thud. Here was one illustration ready-made — when the sudden drops in life occur, it takes more than the cardinal virtues to hold us up. He jotted down a few more leads, then continued reading.)

Part III. Husband and wife and the duties of Christian marriage.

If happiness, harmony, completeness are desired, the " oughts " are of one kind.

If " my way only " is desired, there are no " oughts " save to ignore everyone but self.

Divorces come often because the " oughts " are absent. We make choices for desired ends — different " oughts " for different persons and different situations.

A few illustrations:

An alcoholic and divorce—children; quarrels and divorce; mental cruelty, incompatibility, secret loves; so-called rights.

What do we want? Too often the immediate pleasure without thought of the remote pain.

Seldom are we perplexed when we focus attention on love's meaning, purpose, and end — oneness and devotion.

In other words, marital failure is the fault of refusing to do one's duty.

The Church exists to keep the ideal before us and to help us take the right road and to keep on it. It is so easy to take the eyes off the road and run into the ditch.

Many factors enter in, but for the great mass of us, things can be pinned down to a very small, reasonable, easily remembered compass.

(Parson Jim knew that several other cases of conscience were needed to make this last point more complete. He recalled two cases: one of the doctor who made a fatal mistake because of a sin committed while in medical school; another of a woman whose life was ruined because she felt a little lie never hurt anyone. He'd have to work on these. The conclusion came along finally. Parson Jim hoped his congregation would not feel that " finally " quite so keenly.)

Conclusion. There are always two ways, either right or wrong, or the better of two rights, or the lesser of two evils. There is always a choice to be made, based upon the ends desired.

God is always ready to respond when called on for help in making the decision and carrying it through.

With every choice the process is the same: " Is this right for me now? " Our conception of the end will lead us. " I can make the choice and carry through only by God's help." The Christian will pray to follow the line of duty: " O God, help me to know the right, to desire it, to choose it, and to depend upon thee for seeing it through, no matter what the cost. Amen."

Only man can say and mean and attain: " I want to be a better man." Animals can only follow their urges.

Text: Let us hear the conclusion of the whole matter. Fear God and keep his commandments: for this is the whole duty of man. (Ecclesiastes 12:13)

God's love as revealed in Jesus Christ causes us to fear separation from him and to follow his commands, because we know it is a far better way than any we could devise.

The light flashed on over the door to the pilot's head-quarters in the nose of the plane: " Fasten your safety belts. No smoking, please." Parson Jim put his sermon notes away, fastened his belt and watched the lights below, as the plane banked into the wind for a landing. He was sorry the journey had ended so quickly, but his thoughts on preaching would help materially for as long as he remembered them.

CHAPTER X

RADIO: MEDITATIONS, DEVOTIONS

Think on these things.
PHILIPPIANS 4:8

SEVERAL ILLUSTRATIONS of the type of sermon used in a fifteen-minute Sunday-morning program called " The Miniature Church of the Air " are given. Note the method of analogy. The sermonettes or meditations were designed to capture the listeners, especially men, before they heard the word " sermon " and cut off the radio. Incidentally, this particular series was recorded for " Upstairs Incorporated " to be used in veterans' hospitals over the country.

Ruts

" ' Take care which rut you choose; you will be in it for the next twenty-five miles.'

"A traveler once saw that sign at a crossroad in Canada, when the frost was breaking up. It provides an excellent illustration for the only theory of free will which it seems possible to hold. We know that our wills are not entirely free to make any choice at every point. And to believe that everything is absolutely determined makes nonsense of all that we value in human life. But at points along the road of life there are choices which we can make, and those choices will determine our lives for a certain period, sometimes forever." [1]

At certain times of the year country travelers must deal with ruts — ruts in the road, made by the alternate freezing

[1] By Percy Sylvester Malone. From *The Churchman.* Used by permission.

and thawing, the softening, track-making, hardening process so common, particularly in rural areas. These ruts may prove a bane or a blessing — a bane if they fasten one down to a path which leads where one should not go; a blessing if they keep us on the right road when we may be tempted to go the wrong way.

Ruts are interesting. I cannot help but see the good and the bad points of these grooves, known or unknown, that guide our destinies. When a person says, " He's in a rut," it is not usually complimentary, for he means, " He is doing the same old thing in the same old way; he is following the rut of least resistance; he is unconscious of the growing needs, of the times for readjustment."

Ruts can become the burial place of what were once fresh ideas and ideals. Ruts can take away all desire for achievement and lull one into a false sense of security. Ruts leave us immobile, slow to change, with an eye on the present as the inevitable future. Ruts remained in are sure signs of belief in the impossibility of doing anything about any given situation, a belief that what has always been will always be, and what was good enough for my father is good enough for me.

Jesus came into a world lumbering along in well-defined ruts, political, economic, and religious. The political rut was the domination of Rome. The economic rut was trade with the spice-laden East. The religious rut was the law of tradition. Religion in Jesus' day had followed the Mosaic code for centuries. It had degenerated into a set of rules to keep rather than laws to live by. It had become meticulous subservience to the so-called letter of the law which left much to be desired in the growth of the soul.

Jesus attempted to jar the people out of this rut, unsuccessfully, except for a few who were drawn out of the rut of daily drudgery and set forth to blaze new trails which would lead men to a place closer to the presence of God.

There are several ruts we find today that might be filled in and made decent for Christian travel if we but remembered what Jesus tried to do.

The first one is the rut of tradition. " It has always been done this way," is its infallible authority for existence. Jesus used the rut and also leveled it by making it clear that tradition of itself was no good unless it furnished a foundation and an inspiration upon which to build a more glorious future. A clinging to the things of the past without making them stepping-stones to the future is wasteful. Remember what has been said or done and use it to help fit us for the needs of the present day or point us toward the future. Awe and pride over a forefather should help equip us to be forefathers.

The second one is the rut of the law. " It says so in the statute book — hear these words " is the inevitable citation. Jesus was a bit impatient with anyone who failed to see beneath the outward word into the real human problem the law was intended to solve. Laws are ever transient, but human needs persist. Jesus illustrated time and time again that the law was made for man, not man for the law. No law is adequate now unless it deals with all sides of human need and seeks to meet them.

The third and the last one we shall consider today is the rut of accepting circumstance supinely. " So be it — there is nothing we can do " is its usual wail. Jesus never came to terms with circumstance in the form of compromise or appeasement. He knew that God was still in control of his universe and was still seeing that man was superior to every circumstance, so long as man depended on him. Jesus depended on God and found direction and courage for every crisis, every situation. His policy was: " Come what may, God has an answer for me through me."

Ruts are usually bad ones. But there are occasionally a few good ruts. Sometimes we cannot arrive unless we follow them to our goal.

The first one is the rut of a way made clear for us to follow; a well-defined path set by Jesus.

The second one is the rut of good habits, made firm and sure and automatic by the exercise of spiritual laws.

The third one is the rut of appreciation for the modes of living which have gone before us; making the past push the present along into the future.

Perhaps it would be fairer to call " good " ruts the channels of usefulness leading to accomplishment and advance.

Perhaps it would be truer to call " bad " ruts the wheel-guides to lost initiative, unproductive habits, and stymied mental processes.

Jesus was for the one but against the other. If we are his followers, we shall beware of ruts and look for channels — that the revolving beacon of our lives may become a true guide to a safe landing place for the ship of time.

Bug on a Rug

An adventurous bug once took a journey into the land of the Persian rug. Quite far it was, and tiresome, too, but the little bug was determined to explore this dark continent bordering so temptingly the edge of his existence. A long expanse of shiny floor, then a wilderness of string, until at last, spread farther than his million eyes could see, a fuzzy ocean of smooth soft color. " Well, well, so this is the land of the Persian rug. How flat and uninteresting it seems. I wonder if I shall find it more alluring as I travel along. We shall see." And the bug, after this most illuminating meditation, jogged on. A bright lane of red caught his fancy, and up the lane he went. But, erelong, a patch of brown crossed his path and held him fast. Over the red, which was next to the brown, a delightful green seemed to beckon him on. Then off he went into fields of black and purple and yellow and blue — and he wandered for a day and a night.

"I've had enough of this aimlessness. There is no rhyme, no reason, no thrilling sights, to this talked-of land of my dreams. It is all a jumble. I shall always regret this utter waste of time." And the little bug returned home, without having discovered that this strange country was one of the most beautiful and valuable of the exotic weavings of Persian artists.

No one can become an artist in living without a knowledge of perspective. That is why Jesus dealt daily in the business of lifted-up hearts. Perspective is gained from heights. Jesus' life was a constant sounding of the Sursum Corda — "Lift up your hearts," and putting responses on men's lips — " We lift them up unto the Lord."

The higher we get above the blinding, blurring sensory perceptions of self; the farther removed from the sameness of things; the more we allow our spirits soaring space, the sooner will life become a large thing, with beautiful colors and patterns.

Like the bug, we embark upon life with fresh and eager wonder, with great expectations. But so often, like the bug, we do not find what we saw in our imaginations. We are not grown tall enough or big enough to see things whole, and to relate them.

Yet we give up reluctantly our tight clinging to near-sighted eyes because of preconceived plans and already worked-out patterns. If life is seen as patches of shadows before our eyes, or as blue and brown streaks of unrelenting ugliness here and there, or as a jumble without order and purpose, or as a disillusion which must come to all, what chance has even the intricate and wonderful beauty and pattern of a real Persian rug for our beholding?

Men journey into or toward a promised kingdom of God and see it as the bug saw the rug — they glimpse a vision and thrill to it, but when it fails to materialize, they return to their old ways disconsolate; when all the while they may have been wandering over the outer fringe of the wide expanse of that very kingdom.

Why? It is the last-ditch stand to hold on to *our* way of seeing and doing and believing.

Jesus said:

"I, if I be lifted up." He was lifted up to a high point of personal relationship with God because he relinquished all claim to himself (the self which was capable of only buglike journeying) and allowed God to step in and lift his spirit high above this self to a point where he saw things in perspective. Life began to make sense from this point of view.

When we judge God, the world, life, people, from the bug on the rug position, what chance has even a kingdom of God to show up as a worthy and bountiful perfection attainable in human life? This is essential if we would follow Christ, and comes into actuality when we look up to the good Father, God of love and light and life that lifted him up for men to see and know.

Slow, near-sighted bug on a rug? Far more wonderful a full-grown man, standing tall and strong, fully surrendered and climbing with Christ the steep ascent where man can see in splendor and proper perspective.

Elevators

When I was a teen-age boy, I ran an elevator in a hotel. It was rather interesting for at least six of the twelve hours' daily stint. My greatest sorrow came from having to listen over and over again to the so-called funny remark, usually accompanied by loud laughter, " He has his ups and downs." That was a long time ago, when the body growth was consuming energy that was later diverted to the growth of the mind. But I have been thinking a lot about that well-worn phrase lately and how fitting it is as an analogy for real life. Just for convenience of reference, let us use the same hotel of seven stories where I worked as one who had " his ups and downs."

Strange but true how many of us are jerked up to the seventh floor and dropped down to the basement without ever knowing that floors in between exist. *Up* or *down* describes fairly accurately the major portion of the world's population, neither extreme of which can be predicted very far in advance.

It is always a sign of spiritual infancy, when we find a person who is up when things are going all right and down when going all wrong. In the former state, life is rosy and faith in God is easy. But in the latter state, life is not worth living and faith in God is an illusion; so think the " up-and-downers."

From top floor to basement in recurring cycles is no evidence of a balanced, poised life, sure of its levels of ascent. In between " seven, please " and " all the way down " we find the floors on which the life of the world is lived for both present and future, the present on lower levels, the future on higher ones. Gradual ascent spoils not the view nor the contrast between light and dark.

Jesus warned about staying on the heights, isolated from the other levels. He also warned about staying forever on the lower levels without an occasional trip to the roof for a bit of perspective.

It is all too true that life has its ups and downs. It would be very monotonous if it didn't, but this does not mean the extremes of ups and downs, with the selfishly superior feeling of the one and the lost, inferior feeling of the other.

There is only one height to be concerned about and that is our quiet time on prayer-mountain with God. There is only one depth to be concerned about and that is the dark place of our sin.

Early in religious history man called the one "heaven" and the other "hell."

Despite our sporadic jerks up and drops down, the ultimate aim of all life is to go from bottom to top, a floor at a time, preparing on each one the new demands of the next level. Our stabilizing factor is God. He is our "lift" (an English term for elevator) from one level to the next. He keeps us from slipping, he motivates our climbing to higher levels. Men long to be on top, but usually in terms of success, financially or otherwise. On top, in spiritual terms, means rising above evil and all the lower yearnings of our heritage to a place where they no longer have dominion over us.

All during the coming days, as you ride up and down in elevators, carry on this spiritual analogy with daily life. The motor is God's power. The cable is his tie with man. The cage is life. You are the manipulator or operator. The control handle is prayer. God's elevator is always going up with carrying power for all. Up by the power of God, down only by the power of evil (the devil). The choice is ours. Following God's way is not half so difficult as making a choice of the initial start. Patience is also needed. Elevators are faster than they were, but they are still symbolic of man's ascent Godward; and for our clouded day they are an everlasting sign of God's friendly universe carrying on in orderly fashion the ongoing, upward-moving process of life, developing on every level the strength and stature to lead ever to a higher one — with the goal set as oneness with God.

You will find flaws in the analogy, but be sure your discoveries are not leads toward a way out or a rationalization to hide the few pertinent facts which confront you: namely, that the emotionally unstable person, with his unpredictable spiritual ups and downs, is so because of faith in his poor confused self — hence the fluctuations — instead of the eternal God who never changes. Another fact emerges as valid: namely, that the depths are good only for discovering a height to climb to and never as an abode of the spirit; just as the heights are good only for a glimpse of God and an enlargement of capacities. Living on the levels in between will produce a balance like unto that found in Jesus — humility of what we know we are and strength because of what we know we can be with God's help.

Decide today for the slow, steady trip up and in patience seek the heights, through the levels in between, where our life's end will be another life's beginning. Meditate on the analogy and push the button for " Up."

Story-Books
Of making many books there is no end.
Ecclesiastes 12:12

My paradise is a bookshop, full of bright, fragrant, new books. I cannot resist their allure. It's the same way with a library, with its row upon row upon row of books, the complete record of all phases of life. I suppose this fascination, this passion, was born of love, because I do love books. They have been my intimate friends for many years. They were the make-believe of my childhood, my magic road to happiness. Even now I can conjure up the lovely, fantastic characters of long ago and linger awhile for sheer joy. Then, they were simply boon companions; now I know they were my introduction to life. Yes, life, sometimes disguised but always there. These story-books are still the magic keys to other worlds but in a different way. Maturity has given eyes to my imagination and now I am finding in them sure guides, ideal patterns, much needed reflections — in brief, aids to every step as life goes on.

"Of making many books there is no end." I've often wondered why. I think it is because they record lives, and so long as life continues to be so popular, the clamor for mirrors will never die.

One of the first books to become popular was the Bible, a collection of many books. This great book has become the norm for the Church's life — its book of lives. More people have been influenced by it than any other one book. Why? Just because it has recorded the natural, uncolored lives of men and women, with similar characteristics to ours, and has left very definitely two roads for our choice, the one to follow and the other to avoid. Moses, Samuel, Elijah, Elisha, Amos, Hosea, Jeremiah, Ezekiel, Ezra, Nehemiah, Jesus, Paul, and their kindred host, all lived great lives but not always perfect ones, except Jesus; and they have been recorded for us that we might learn what they knew of God, of life, of man; how they lived, met their problems, and how they died. The chief value of the Bible is that we may see how they approximated the perfect child of God. But most of us have learned little of the Bible's wonders. The Church, having based its all on this book, is concerned with life, mainly with *a life* — Jesus' — which touches all life. That is why she is interested in story-books, because that's what a story-book really is, the record of a life touching all lives within its reach, influencing them for good or for ill. We shall gain by studying the book, the writers, and the men whose lives are recorded there.

It must be fascinating to write a book, to feel the warmth and power which come from directing a group of souls through the intricate relations of life. Many of us have dreamed of writing a book, and when that ambition was not realized, have forgotten the desire. We seldom realize that all of us *can* write books, *are* writing books: autobiographies of which we are the authors and for which we are totally responsible. Chapter by chapter each one takes its form, being written slowly but surely for the library of time. The setting is there: a country village, a small town, a teeming city. The characters, too: hero and villain, family and friends. Likewise the plot, which develops as we go along. Incidents of failure, success, happiness, tragedy, sorrow, love, hate, follow in rapid succession. Some will like the book, others will not. Many will criticize, some will defend. At times it will be dull and slow, at other times racing madly along with emotion and excitement. Yes, we are each one writing a book, which is the only record we leave behind; and that means we are writing our immortality daily, with each indelible stroke of our pen.

Our book will fall into one of three classes:

Those destined for a future glory;

Those destined to be lost in oblivion; and

Those that will become the guides and inspiration for those following after. How often have we thought or heard, " I want to be like him." It is an absorbing task, placing letters of black on pages of white, conscious all the time that there can be no erasures, but that there can be change of direction toward a different ending.

I recall the weekly essay I used to write for my church bulletin. The copy was prepared on an indelible carbon and you could not remove a mistake conveniently. I would get an idea, start at the top, and if the typewriter slipped, I changed the meaning to follow suit and wound the whole thing up at the bottom of the page, sometimes far removed from the original idea. That is almost like our autobiographies. We cannot remove the mistakes — which, by the way, are simply the necessary ways of learning how — but we can rearrange and compensate for them. No two of our books are exactly alike, but all are made out of the fabric of life's richness and life's poverty. Indifferent authors produce indifferent books. That is one reason for the Church's existence: to inspire concern in each human heart about the book he is writing and to help the result to be more like the perfect Godlike life of Jesus. And no matter how scanty or commonplace a life seems, it possesses inherently sufficient material for a masterpiece. *All* lives are interesting, for truth is indeed stranger than fiction. How often the unreality of some incident makes us remark, " Why, it's just like a movie or a novel." We cannot believe it has happened. I can remember several events which could not have happened, but did. Daily incidents lend charm to the plot, but our reactions to these incidents furnish the spiritual power. We must always be the hero, in the sense of carrying the greater responsibility. The ending may not always be happy, but happy or sad, those qualities of courage and greatness which make a hero must be evident. That is the most important thing to remember, for each book will be read and judged by God and by man, whether it was guided and inspired by God or by man. And this last is the crux of our story and of our lives — guided and inspired by God, not man alone.

Our chief inspiration and constant reminder that our story-books must be the finest of all literature is the knowledge that we are the schools in which the children of the world learn to write the stories of their lives. *We* are the books *they* read. We are literally their textbooks. We must be the type of hero who never lets them down, never disillusions them. Their hero need not always be rich and handsome but he must always be kind and lovable. We must show them in great detail the Life which has made our lives what they are, must show them the Christ who made our way clear to the end.

Which brings us to the close, with a quiet prayer for story-books — your story-books and mine, both of them belonging to God — and with the fervent wish that you will discover and absorb into your own creation the finest things contained in all the books you read and see; and may the story of Jesus find its dominantly proper place.

Crystal Globes That Shatter

One Saturday evening in deep midwinter, I sat in Orchestra Hall in the city of Chicago in my season's seat and listened to Tchaikowsky's last and greatest symphony. Upon the surge and passion of that tremendous music, my soul was lifted as in chariots of flame through storm and darkness, up and on to the grandeur of great spaces, like the spaces between the stars, where my spirit knew itself transcendent and triumphant over all fleeting and transitory things. But even as I listened, in the rapt sublimity of that mighty music, half heard there crept in now and then the echoes from the street outside. And when at length the symphony was finished, and through the open doors of the building I went out into the roar of the actual world, to the rumble and clatter of the elevated overhead, the clash of gears in automobiles, the clang of gongs on streetcars, and all the thousand-tongued bedlam of the street, it was as though that mighty other world of imagination had suddenly been shattered like a crystal globe beneath an avalanche of stones. My emotionally inflated imagination had been basking in a borrowed kind of radiance never really my own.

When such radiance comes in unrestrained abundance and finds itself so easily shattered, we are dealing with the fragile stuff of the unenduring and the transitory. The truly great moments of life are like crystal globes for most of us, elusive and fragile, and when broken are beyond repair. But even though some have held such lovely crystal globes for only a moment and lost them, others greater and more completely in control have clung to them successfully.

What is the secret, then, of this possession of great moments, of greatness? Why could Tchaikowsky write without the disturbances of the world seeping in to distract him? Why could he nail down his sounds with the spikes of immortality? Why can't we all hold on to life's great moments? Why do they slip so easily away? Why does the outside world enter in and shatter our little world of beauty, loveliness, and happiness? Why does our hard-earned radiance change to gloom at the slightest touch or tingle?

We cannot answer the "why" of genius, but we can quote an answer from Edwin Arlington Robinson's *Matthias at the Door:* "I have found gold where you found gravel, and I can't give it to you. I feel and see it, but you must find it somehow for yourself. It's not negotiable." [1] These deepest experiences are seldom explainable or transferable, but when really our own, they change us and abide with us and transmute us eternally.

Religion is man's deepest possible experience. Does it offer unshatterable crystal globes for the holding? Jesus proved it did and does. His life is the perfect example. No factor of the world's clatter, whether of sound or of deed, could touch its anchorage to eternal values, all God-given. Note the last week, the last day of his life. They had no power to affect his inner possession of God's radiance. It was there undisturbed in the midst of violent storm and noise-making. His crystal globe did not shatter. If the world disappoints our hold upon reality, or makes us uncertain of

[1] From *Matthias at the Door*. Copyright, 1931, by Edwin Arlington Robinson. Reprinted by permission of The Macmillan Company, publishers.

it; if our so-called religion does not hold us up in time of stress, we need to seek deeper and to work harder at the task of discovering God, with Jesus close at hand as guide and helper, in order to earn that which the world cannot take away or disappoint or even ruffle for one brief moment.

Radiance one minute and gloom the next is not religion, but an emotional desire come true at both extremes. After a beautiful service with music and atmosphere just right, we are usually lifted up, but too often only by the shatterable crystal globe of emotion. Emotion is not of itself religion, and if left alone with nothing added, or if not trained to a higher end and purpose, leads nowhere and disappears at the slightest jar or push. The same thing is true of sentimentality.

Remember the sadness of Jesus at the falling away, the desertion of the disciples when the way became too hard for them, when they did not understand enough to walk courageously where he led. I think of our own tendency to fall away, to desert because it is so difficult, because it requires so much to make permanent the unshatterableness of our crystal globes. Anything that lasts forever is a part of God's religion and worth our all, but like great music, it must possess us to remain ours forever. Keep your crystal globes of reality of the Christian religion bright and clear, so full of real radiance that they will be untouched and unshattered by the intrusion of the harsh hate and fleeting impermanence of all lesser things. Cling tenaciously to that crystal globe of religion (that which binds us securely to God, whatever comes) fashioned and formed and lived by Jesus, which inspires and lifts and empowers our never-ending progress toward the health and happiness and completeness of life.

This globe will never shatter, but will always reflect God's way for us, as we hold it close and gaze into its clear shining depths.

The Parable of the Artascope

It was a cold evening and I had driven far to pay a call on a wayward family in my parish. A great hubbub of excitement greeted my entrance. The whole family was grouped together in the living-room in front of the fire; my coming had interrupted an apparently absorbing occupation in which they were engaged. The most conspicuous object in the room was a card table, a bit rickety under one corner, piled high with clutterings of junk — bits of wire, straw, tin foil, colored cloth, and colored paper all jumbled together in wild confusion. Arising out of the chaos was a peculiar-looking instrument, triangular in shape, looking almost like a microscope.

The eldest daughter, noticing my interest, dragged me over, pushed me into a chair, and bade me look into the instrument. She immediately placed a few of the odds and ends on the little revolving table directly underneath the long slender triangle.

It seemed silly to me to be peering through a triangle, merely to gaze at a few discarded scraps, but gaze I did and to my utter amazement the most wonderful sight greeted my eyes. Lo, and behold, with the magic of a Cinderella godmother, those lowly fragments were changed to colored jewels, sparkling designs ever changing, ever new, as the little table moved slowly around. I was enchanted. Ugly bits, useless things, were snatched up eagerly and aimlessly and placed under the spell of the magic wand. Again and again I witnessed the miraculous transformation.

I asked what it was called. "Artascope" was the reply. Artascope — what an idea! And so there grew the parable of the artascope.

The artascope had truly opened for me a parable of life. Here I discovered an analogy for the secret of how ugliness,

confusion, and waste could be changed like the many pieces
on the table, under the magic touch of love, understanding,
and intent concern. How like ourselves the remnants on the
table were; how like God's ways was the artascope. Yes,
like the artascope, God gives meaning, design, and holiness
to the tattered remnants of life. It was not so much the
instrument itself that captivated and inspired me, but the
idea behind it. I like to think of its inventor as being one
who had lived among sordid things, ash heaps, in smelly
tenements, in sunless alleys, who lifted up his eyes, his mind,
and his heart, dreaming and scheming how to make things
more beautiful. Once again it brings us to God the Creator,
who had the same idea. The Spirit of Christ was his artascope, through which men could see life, *can* see life transformed.

As we look around and observe our fellow men, we find
our impressions of them to be similar to mine of the table —
a mass of poor tags and rags who bring forth unthinking
judgment from our lips. But perhaps our judgments are
distorted; perhaps every class of humankind seems to every
other class nothing but flotsam and jetsam. Jesus as a man
saw the flaws and weaknesses of man, but Jesus as God saw
more, much more, and through him we may learn spiritual
discernment. The artascope is the instrument of spiritual
discernment, the instrument of holiness. If used before
judging and forming pictures, both the judging and the
pictures will be changed through the Spirit of Christ. We
find in them through him the measure of every man's true
worth, be it attained or potential. The disciples, as they
caught and dispensed some of his Spirit, occasionally saw
things in their loveliness. The men who condemned the
woman taken in adultery dropped their stones as they found
themselves in his presence. Zacchaeus, under the spell of his
influence, turned completely around in his purpose. Instead

of money gained as his life's goal, life given for Christ to use became the joy-song of the changed Zacchaeus. The artascope might well be, instead of a childish toy, the instrument of second sight, the look-once-again that could change the errors and flaws which our human judgment discerns, and help us to see the potential value of every person for whom Christ died. Man's greatness awaits discovery. Our use of the artascope may lead another to his real self — may lead to the discovery of our own selves.

Once again let us look back at the table. As I contemplate it, I can see bits of self spread over it like the parts of an old clock, torn down by some boyish hand. I can almost identify each disjointed part — tasks, dreams, failures, fears, phobias, disillusionments, sins, ideas, knowledge, courage, ambitions — the very hodgepodge of individual existence. It is a bit discouraging to see such poor material for reconstruction. I see further: resignation, complexes, fate, dullness, oblivion. But wait; we have forgotten the artascope. Let us use it. Just as we knew, all is changed. We are put into immediate relationship with the highest, and through the artascope, which is the Spirit of Christ, we find we can tackle the mess and find it not hopeless; plan and pattern begin to bring order from confusion, and from the discarded and the ash heap there comes a possible new and more wonderful life for every man. Just as the artascope can be used to transform discarded scraps, so the Spirit of Christ must be the medium to turn our dreams and our resolutions into miracles. When we look at him, turn to him, and follow where he leads, life becomes as different as the jumbled junk does under the magic of the artascope.

*   *   *

Here are several examples of the daily meditation-devotion type of broadcast used daily for six years, in Richmond, Virginia, and for one year in Lexington, Kentucky. This program, known as " Haven," had as its chief aim the coming into homes daily to stimulate individual and family devotional life.

Discipline

" Discipline " is a familiar word to most of us. It has many meanings, but today let us take this area-defining description: " Discipline is the chalkline drawn by God's Spirit to control man's walking in the way." As we plan the route of a new-found life-to-be, we are grateful for the discipline which acts as a centering white line, visible at every curve and in any light. Discipline is the willingness to be circumscribed in order to find a greater freedom. We mention a few of the difficult disciplines — difficult at first because they involve breaking in new habits foreign to a lax, spoiled mind: getting up a few moments earlier, for example, every day in the week; facing facts as they come, with no delay at all; making the immediate choice of the right thing, no matter what desire says, without haggling and hedging.

Discipline is the cure for self-indulgence or any other form of selfishness, because it requires living in accordance with an established code. It is not easy. That is why people shun it. Their vision is not yet adequate for the trials of the journey until they accept literally Jesus' words, " Take my yoke upon you, and learn of me." His yoke is the discipline which holds us to the essential learning from him about God, which will remove the burden of sin and shame from our hearts. His yoke is God's will for us and our willingness to submit to it.

I repeat, it is hard. No easy-going response or half-hearted attempt will do — it is all or nothing. Christ asks such complete obedience to discipline because " he knows that in this way only can we find the fullness of life and joy and peace, and be at one with his purpose for the world."

Any decision to follow Christ from now on must be made with " eyes open both to the loveliness of God and also to the great demands he will make on us." We must see the loveliness of God and of his purpose, for that alone will keep us steadfast and make us ready to meet his demands. The fact, of course, is that whatever we have to face — difficulties, hardships, rough places and utter darkness — he is by our side, bearing the load with us, encouraging and cheering us on. So can we fulfill our nature, for which we have been born into his family, for we shall be playing our part in his scheme of things. The road will be difficult, but we shall help each other, and find the fullness of life.

The plan of the route is Christ's, not ours. We cannot expect it to be any easier than his was. But when we say, " Lead and I will follow," we know he will be there to carry us through.

Discipline means a moment-by-moment consciousness of what God wants of us, expects of us, with every avenue open for our immediate recognition of it, to the exclusion of the old " I want."

Yielding to the absorbing idea of God-control will insure freedom from reaction to personal and world problems in a distorted and exaggerated emotional way. Emotional balance, directed and controlled judgment result from the discipline imposed upon every disciple. " Know thyself " in relation to God and man, but do not fool thyself that thou art God and all men.

How long ago has it been since you gave up that eagerly accepted discipline of the newborn life? It must be followed day by day. There is no other way. With never a let-down, never a let-up, never an unyoking for a spiritual rest. The discipline of keeping near God through Christ can never be relaxed. Yoked for life to his life we find life. Anything less is compromise and will lead to disillusionment.

Conversion

Conversion is usually a day-by-day growth and expansion along the lines of living with Christ, laid down as Godlike. As men have been penetrated by the Spirit of Christ and have seen the richness of his perfect life, and have longed after it because it was so much more wonderful than anything they had ever known, they have cried out, " Master, we would follow thy way; teach us and show us." And Jesus always speaks these familiar words in answer, " I am the way, the truth, and the life; no man cometh unto the Father but by me."

Therefore, we start with Christ and end with God, and in between we give up all desire and claim to the old person so long in control of our rather miserable destiny. When Christ is brought into the picture and set clearly in front of us, his very person inspires us to leave all and follow him.

Most of us hunger and thirst after His life and way, and earnestly pledge ourselves to give up the sorry and fruitless bypaths we have been traveling. But the moment we strike a familiar temptation we find desire is not enough, and that we must literally lay hold on God and use his strength at every point of our weakness. Likewise, exposure to Christ is not always enough. Our deepest sin-habits are difficult to deal with and it takes, almost always, the crucifying experience of an uprooted " I " to loose their tenacious hold upon us. Men usually consciously begin their conversion at some particular point of weakness or block or blindness. Here is the point of their desperation and admitted limitation. The battle begins on this front. Victory here spells hope for final victory in the war within, between the forces of evil.

Our handbook and guide in this process is the New Testament, which we must read and study. Just as in the Bureau of Standards in Washington we find the standards for every measurement of distance and weight, so in the New Testament we find standards for every measurement of moral and spiritual doubt. As we learn more of Jesus in the gospels and in the letters of Paul, we shall become more and more certain of the Christ whose perfection and possession of eternal treasures always keeps us moving toward him as the goal of the most satisfying and perfect life in this, God's own world. By this sign and in this life we can have our lives made over in the face of moral failure and defeat, moral degradation and disgust, moral weakness and shame.

If! Now that little word must enter. Whenever anyone paints an alluring picture of something to be obtained, we grow a bit suspicious and wait for the climax, the cost. The cost of Christ-likeness begins at the point of *if*. If we would make the plunge and follow, not far off, but close by his side, we must be willing to go all the way and engage in whatever spiritual discipline is necessary to clear the trail back and to take the trail forward.

Turn to Paul's letter to the Romans, chapter 7, verses 18-25. There is where we begin: acknowledging our sin and recognizing that in Jesus we can be saved. Continue in the same letter with chapter 8, verses 1-17. Then, be very quiet for awhile and begin to list these sins you acknowledge. Write them down. Nothing which blocks our way to God through Christ is too small to jot down — especially every sin-describing word with the prefix " self."

The camera is grinding today, taking a picture of each " I." If there is not time enough in the morning to complete the list, work at it during the day in spare moments. Bring that long list of unloveliness back with you tomorrow morning and remember in this letter of Paul is found the hope of a dawn to come.

Where Is Their God?

What is the Bible? We answer immediately: words of faith from the past of man's seeking and finding; the Word of God as set forth by Israel's peers. Bible means "the books"; in reality, a "library" of many books. The Holy Bible is the record of the revelation of God, as expressed by man. It was compiled and put forth by the church. But remember that the church was at work for many years before the limits of the Old Testament were decided upon and while the New Testament was being written. Keep the origins straight — first Christ, then the church, then the Bible. Every Christian church uses the Bible as the source book of Christian truth. Public services of worship are built around it. Sermons are preached from it. Church people should be at home with it. Christ is our Lord and the Bible presents him.

Man must first find God in the low places before ascent is made. This is true of all the ages of his development as well as any one age of it. The Bible would never have been written unless man had discovered God, bit by bit; unless man had engaged in the never-ending quest for answers to the great questions of life and death, many of which are still unknown; unless he had desired to preserve what others had discovered of God, and to express, as best he could in mere words, his innermost experiences of God. The Bible pictures the dawn of man's consciousness of something yet to be attained, as he took his first step upward from his animal heritage. When man built his first altar, which acknowledged this greatness yet to be, he distinguished himself from his forebears. In this origin of man's primitive seeking after a god who could and would answer his questions, we must never forget, is written the approach to the God almost every man in every age finds necessary. This makes the

Bible an essential tool today. For is it not the record of the beginning of man's ascent toward God as he was able to understand? So today, as we are able to understand, wonders will happen in the darkness of our ignorance.

Man gradually found God, the source of life's power, and passed the findings on from generation to generation in stories which have never grown old or outmoded in their essential truth.

Take Joel 2:12-17, for example. The passage tells how in the time of great national crisis — for them it was the ravages of a locust plague and drought, which meant impending famine — there arose a man who brought them out of their hopelessness of darkness and gloom once again into the indomitable spiritual hope that was the soul of Judaism. Joel got down to basic facts. We must combat the enemy by repentance for our lack of faith and our wringing of hands, and seek God's forgiveness and direction as to what to do in this time of peril. Rending your garments will avail nothing. Rend your hearts in the anguish of repentance and turn once again to the Lord your God.

Through the ages, the Bible has picked up and imprisoned the actual experiences of men faced with dilemma after dilemma, only to find the mountains leveled and the rough places made smooth, as they have turned once again from dependence upon themselves to the source of all power, God himself.

People are questioning in their minds as they look at Christians today and are asking this question propounded long ago, in Joel, "Where is their God?" That question will remain unanswered until we who believe in God take him out of the pages of a book and follow his will for us.

Worship

This is " Haven," coming to you for the first time on the day of the Sun. We have two responsibilities today. The first is to keep our continuity with those who cannot attend church. The second is to call those who can attend church to worship in one somewhere today.

" The hour cometh, and now is, when the true worshippers shall worship the Father in spirit and in truth: for the Father seeketh such to worship him." (John 4:23)

Almost instinctively we are called, through the age-long custom of church-going, to worship God in a church once a week. There are few who hear my voice now who are not planning to go to church at least once this day. It is easy to worship God on Sunday, when the very air is laden with chimes and bells and the quietness associated with the Lord's Day. It was ingrained in me from my childhood, and if I did not attend church on Sunday, the day just wasn't complete for me. It is natural for us to worship God, to indulge in a display of worth-ship; that is, to express the quality of the value of God to us, to express our worth to him.

Everywhere there is always devotion to what is believed to be of great value. That is why people worship. Because through worship the supreme values of religion become intelligible even to the meanest capacity and are rendered discernible in contemporary interests and problems. Finding God in the actual world in which people live means a vital religion.

Half of worship is the worth we find. The other half is the expression of that found worthy. " Showing forth our praise not only with our lips but in our lives." Therefore, it is the technique for harmonizing God and man, for man worships only as he has full realization of God's presence.

It is the expression of a consciousness, a love, a recognition of the Person of God.

Instinctively we seek God's house on Sunday morning. We heed the call of worship. This is essential for Christians. Christianity is a fellowship and each service of worship acts as a reminder, exists to recall, aids to refresh man's daily duty to God. It is the source where we find common aspiration and inspiration, courage and hope, instruction and help; where our attitudes are conditioned, our perspective cleared, our fears and doubts overcome.

But it is not a cloistered thing. We may worship where we are, we may worship as we walk, as we live with and dwell among men. Worship, again, is the complete fulfillment of religion — *religare*, a binding together — the constant contact between all angles of the triangle. All true religion is triangular; you and others form the base, God forms the apex. Our experience of God is bound up inextricably with our human relationships.

If we are living in touch with God and man, we worship. "If your shoe has a hole in it, my foot is cold." We are as interrelated as that. Worship, then, includes values possessed from God, then shared with others — literally carried to them as in a ship.

They that worship God in spirit and in truth, that is, with their entire being all of the time, discovering more and more of the truth, will find the fruits of true worship.

First of all, worship helps us to know God. We come closer to him. We talk with him. He talks with us. Frequently this must be in church. Radio worship is helpful, but it lacks the dynamic of human fellowship which is so contagious. The hour cometh, daily in prayer and meditation, weekly in a tangibly expressed sharing with the triangle.

Secondly, it helps us to know ourselves. Some time ago

a book was published titled, *Man, the Unknown*. The root of most of our modern problems is man's ignorance of himself. In worship we are in the presence of God. Jesus is the mirror we use to see ourselves as we really are. As we lay our lives alongside of his, all of our sins and weaknesses become glaringly apparent — but also our kinship to the divine. Knowledge of God and of self comes through worship.

Thirdly, it helps us to know each other. This completes the triangle. It makes us socially sensitive. We remember the needs of others, our responsibility for helping, and the misfortune of each becomes the experience of all. I think specifically this morning of the suffering in Europe and the appeals which all of us will answer.

Going to worship in church is not enough. "I must worship." Singing psalms and hymns and spiritual songs is not enough. "I must be inspired and motivated in Christian conduct and character." I must have a "satisfying experience of self-dedication and adoration for the glory of God."

At its best and truest, worship seems to me to be direct, vital, joyous, personal experience and practice of the presence of God.

The call to worship may be the sound of bells ringing peals of welcome or the relaxed quiet of a holy day. But whatever be its sounding call in your heart, know that the true worshiper finds the fruits of his worship in a deeper sense of God's guiding presence, a surer instinct of what he is and must become, and a love and appreciation for those who make it possible for him to bring forth the fruits of his redemption.

May God bless you and the day through you, and may he bring you safely into another dawn.

CHAPTER XI

A FEW REMNANTS

Being born again . . . by the word of God,
which liveth and abideth for ever.
I PETER 1:23

T HIS CHAPTER offers a few general comments on some remaining types of writing and speaking, such as conducting retreats, leading conferences, holding missions, preaching Lenten series; also on conducting schools of prayer and religion, addressing civic clubs and groups, special preparation for national and religious occasions, and for every other time when, as Alexander Pope put it, with " Fire in each eye, and papers in each hand, they [the clergy] rave, recite, and madden round the land." We can summarize the general approach; and we can furnish the design and the thread, the needle and the canvas, for another sampler.

The theme. The *leitmotiv.* This should be attractive and compelling and suited to the group we are to address. No fisherman would think of using the same bait for every fish. So we must choose the theme to fit the group. Clergymen will respond to one kind of subject, laymen to another; church women will flock to hear one describing their interest, clubwomen will need something else; and of course secular groups, all the way from the P. T. A. to the Kiwanis Club, will demand a totally different lure. I have known the following subjects to attract the particular group indicated by parentheses: " The Man Who Wanted to Know " (men); " Is God on Vacation? " (church women); "A Feather Bed of Words " (clergymen); " Some Modern Substitutes for Christianity " (clubwomen); " The Child

226

and the Twig Both Bend" (P. T. A.); "Ministers and Strait Jackets" (Kiwanis); "Advance Into Light" (Lenten series); "This Much and More" (teaching or preaching mission); and so on. But take care the subject is more than mere bait; keep to it and don't, as is so often done, depart from it the moment it is announced.

The aim. Put it clearly before you. The reason so many public utterances never seem to get anywhere is that the speaker doesn't know quite where he is going. No one would set out on a long automobile journey today without a plainly marked map of the exact route to take to the destination. The same applies to every talk, long or short. Unless we can summarize the point, what we are aiming to get across, to accomplish, we shall probably never reach a single soul — save only as God uses even our feebleness and our mistakes sometimes to arouse a smoldering flame. Before any writing is done, the condensation of the aim should be set as a masthead at the very top of the page. It should guide every step of the preparation and the final delivery.

The outline. In detail. I've never liked to do this. It is a lot of painstaking work. But it makes the rough places plain and the structure will be less likely to fall under the weight of the added words. Not only this, but the points come readily to mind, and the good outline helps free us from the manuscript, once we are before our congregation or audience. An outline is worth all the time we spend on it, whether to keep our points in proper proportion or to space our illustrations or to guide the way through the maze of our miscellaneous material to the realization of our aim.

The resources. Explore them rather than simply scan hurriedly. Take accurate notes of what you find. All useful quotes should be carefully noted for credit. One of the many temptations which beset a clergyman is to lift outline, illustrations, whole sections from someone else's printed sermon, and use them as one's own. A few with "photographic" memories do it quite unconsciously and reproduce an entire sermon read or heard, with every comma in its proper place. Some rationalize their behavior by declaring they improve on the other man's sermon. But rarely can we do an adequate job with another man's sermon even if we give him the credit.

God has given us a mind and presumably a call to preach his word as it comes to us. We shall stultify our gifts, meagre though they may be, unless we do the best we can with what we have. By all means read sermons for inspiration and jot down apt illustrations, unusual texts, and potent ideas, but grind them into your own brand before attempting any distribution. Be sure of your facts and your meanings — scriptural, scientific, etymological, or personal.

The length. Suit to the time available. One of the greatest of clerical sins (and bad manners) is out-talking the clock — when allowed thirty minutes, to take an hour. Whether we have a day, an hour, or ten minutes, it is far better to stop a few minutes sooner than expected rather than to go overtime even a second. Our generation is clock-minded. Since the radio has taught us the value of seconds, the wise speaker will not ignore them as they tick past. Only by very careful preparation, and in some instances by actual timing beforehand, can we be sure of our termination on time. Leave the listeners wanting more, not applauding because at long last the flow of words has ended.

The writing. The bones with flesh adorned. When a group sees the bones, your message is too thin, too starved. The ribs must never show unless you want to lose your listeners. Very few of us can exist on an outline alone. We must fashion our phrases and sentences upon it. Our style is important; indeed, it is the one thing which marks us off from anyone else. The English language is a marvel of power when used rightly, with beauty, dignity, easy flow, and sharp contrast. But this takes the endless work of word selection, of correct grammar, of transition, of length, of paragraphs and illustrations, of going over and over the manuscript until it hangs together as a literary whole and sounds forth as proper dissonance and cadence to the listening ear. I know you are a busy man, but God is judged by every word which proceedeth out of our mouths.

The delivery. This will vary according to the time and the place and the group. Sometimes it will be formal, from full notes. At other times informal, filling in from an outline. Even the use of the voice will vary from the quiet conversational tone for small groups to the full-throated power necessary in a large auditorium. Keep the hearers in view and never focus attention on the rafters or the spider web in the back corner of the ceiling. One of our great needs is to cultivate the proper use of the voice. When defects of speech cut us off from the ones we would reach, we should leave no stone unturned to remedy the defect. One petition which should be included in every clerical litany is: Good Lord, deliver us from the ministerial voice, with its pious sound, its pompous inflection, its infallible roll of thunder, or operatic singsong. Amen.

The fruit. "By their fruits ye shall know them." The scientific evaluation of the results of any utterance is difficult. But believe your wife before you do your devoted and elderly members.

Of course, quite often it is impossible to know what has happened to those who have heard your message. All of us have been cheered when months or even years later someone tells us of the value of a word we have uttered which had found lodgment and response in them.

The used material. Usually we want to crumple it up and

throw it away, never desiring to see it again. But it is a good idea to keep sermons and talks on file for several years at least, as a kind of chart of progress, and survey of our limitations. Also, when getting ready for some series away from home base, many of these manuscripts will save valuable time, as we find them fitting together and affording an easily re-shaped substance for using again. Occasionally requests for copies will come. It is a simple job to draw the manuscript from the file and type off a copy; then to check it so there will be no mistakes.

What I have written I have written.
JOHN 19:22

Much more needs to be done before we make the ink flow freely into a word which is catching to the eye and will make the air vibrate with a sound which is catching to the ear, and the whole of our written and spoken word function as life action in hearts and minds. Unless we utter words that reveal careful thought and preparation, our mutterings will be without the power and inspiration for bringing about revolutionary change in human life. Let us continue to thank God for his unspeakable gifts of boundless expression; and with humility never cease to ask him to use our voices as his voice and our pens as his instrument for the growth of God's kingdom on earth.

They cry, " Sir, we would see Jesus." (John 12:21) They, the people, ask for bread, the bread of life. They thirst as well as hunger for the well of water springing up within unto eternal life. We are chosen to feed them, to quench their thirst, to show them the Master — his words and his life. We shall fail in these tasks unless the earthen vessels of mind and voice reflect, in so far as they can, the life-changing Spirit of Christ and lead all who freely come " to an inheritance incorruptible, and undefiled, and that fadeth not away." (1 Peter 1:4)